Front cover.

Bert Upson was born at Stoke Ash in 1905. He began farm work at thirteen, his wages of ten shillings (50p.) a week rising to thirty shillings a week by the time he was twenty-one. In 1957 he became a forestry worker and in his retirement he is working as a part-time gardener at Shrubland Hall.

Photography: Mark and Elizabeth Mitchels.

Cover design by Harvey Lawrence-Clegg

EAST ANGLIAN
TALES

EAST ANGLIAN TALES

by
H. Mills West

COUNTRYSIDE BOOKS
NEWBURY, BERKSHIRE

First Published in 1983
by Barbara Hopkinson Books
© H. Mills West 1983
This edition published 1989

COUNTRYSIDE BOOKS
3 CATHERINE ROAD
NEWBURY, BERKSHIRE

ISBN 1 85306 066 6

Produced through MRM Associates, Reading
Printed in England by J.W. Arrowsmith Ltd., Bristol

Foreword

Like many others of his generation, H. Mills West left his local elementary school at fourteen and went to work on the land. After a few weeks he went back to his headmaster to borrow text-books and for the next seven years pored over such mixed learning as these and others provided after the day's manual work was done.

At twenty-one he was offered a place at a small college for agricultural workers, endowed by a well-known firm. The college provided what was then a rare opportunity for young countrymen hungry for knowledge to acquire a broad-based knowledge of the world about them. Then it was back to the land and to the resumed routine of University Extension courses and such classes until a teacher shortage at the end of the war allowed him to qualify for admission to a training college — just twenty years after leaving school.

For twenty five years, H. Mills West taught in country schools the local children for whom he had so much affection and at the same time indulged his memory in recalling and writing down something of the lives and characters of people he had known in early life. From a mass of cuttings of articles and stories published in a variety of newspapers and journals have been chosen the pieces that form this present collection.

"*Let not ambition mock their useful toil,*
Their homely joys, and destiny obscure;
Nor grandeur hear with a disdainful smile,
The short and simple annals of the poor."

Thomas Gray 1716-1771

Contents

Several of these tales have appeared over the years in the
East Anglian Daily Times or the Eastern Daily Press.

A Summer's Evening

The day that young Freddy Broom came home drenched from the mill pond was one of a golden September long ago. He came home like a drowned rat in the afternoon sun, shrinking past the cottages in the back lane, white and scared stiff from the shock of struggling for his life in the water. Worse, however, was to come. His mother was waiting for him beside the gate, fierce with anxiety. He ducked past quickly, knowing the warning signs but was not fast enough to avoid the stinging clout that landed on his ear.

"That's jest to go on with," she promised him bitterly. "I'll git yar father t' give yew a throshin' yew 'ont forgit, when he come hoom. Oh, my word, Freddy —" and all the anger was gone and she was sobbing, dabbing her face hurriedly with the corner of her apron, "— yew worry the insides out o' me, that yew dew."

Freddy got quickly upstairs to dry himself. Then he lay on the bed, on the modest quilt of coloured patches that his mother had made and watched how the long shafts of sunlight patterned the white-washed walls and showed up the scripture texts hanging above the wash-stand. When his father came heavy-footed up the narrow stairs at tea-time, he could hear his mother's shrill voice from down below in the kitchen:

"Yew put yar belt to that boy, Sam. He's got so he don't take a mite o' notice what anyone say ter him. One o' these days he'll git inter real trouble ef yew let him hev his head like yew hev done . . ."

1

His father came in and shut the door and the voice died away. His father was rough and awkward in the small room as though he were too long used to the hard, open life of field and farmyard to feel comfortable in such a small, neat space. He was lost when he had nothing for his hands to do and he bent his head to look out of the window to the familiar fields outside.

"Well, what ha' yew bin up tew, Freddy?" he asked at last, barely hiding the friendly banter in his voice. "Why, yew ain't hardly out o' one scrape afore yew git in another. That worry yar mother, boy, d'ye see?" He paused and added confidingly: "She forgit we was all young once — an' that ain't all that time ago neither."

Freddy watched his father expectantly, as sharp as any wild thing for any sign that might allow him to escape outdoors again, following his father's eyes as he looked down out of the window on to the yard and the garden languishing in the autumnal peace. In the open space where the kennel stood, the dog Floss was showing only her nose and her paws to the sun. Beside the kennel was the battered old chopping block.

"I don't reckon that'd hu't yew a mite," his father decided at last, "to git the rest o' them faggots chopped up. That oughter keep yar fingers out o' mischief for a bit. Yew chop up them faggots an' pack the sticks tidy in the shod. An' don't yew go outer that gate afore yore finished."

He lifted the latch of the door and went out. As he did so the shrill, anxious voice began again: "Hev yew leathered him, Sam? Yew know yore tew sorft wi' that boy —" Momentarily before the door closed Freddy saw his father's face harden and he seemed to go swiftly down the stairs and a chair scraped violently across the floor

2

below as they began another of their bitter quarrels.

Freddy pulled on an old pair of dry corduroys and went down to the yard. He could no more see himself spending a whole evening cutting sticks than sitting down to knit. In a frantic haste he set upon the faggots with the blunted chopper as if they could be made to disappear from the sheer speed of his attack. Sticks flew everywhere. Some thumped the side of the kennel and made poor Floss withdraw even further from sight. At six o'clock, just as he realised that he was getting blisters, his mother came out with some old gloves and two thick slices of bread and jam. She did not speak and Freddy could see that she had been crying.

As soon as he had eaten the jam, Freddy set to again and by seven o'clock the pile of faggots was almost done. Frantic because the sun was already dipping low in the sky, Freddy finished them off in great haste and piled the cut sticks untidily in the shed. His father came out from the cottage and clucked and shook his head sadly at what he saw.

"That's a botched-up job an' no mistake," he said. "But there — I s'pose yew ha' done what I arst. Trouble is yore allust in sich a'mighty hurry. Well, here y'are. I reckon, like anyone else yew got the right to be paid. That's twopence — now put that chopper away an' try an' keep outer any more trouble."

"Can I go out?" asked Freddy, in an itch to get out of the gate into the lane before the sun sank. As his father considered, his mother came out and stood in silence.

"I reckon yew could take Floss for a bit of exercise," his father decided. His mother's voice was not shrill any more but hard and firm. "I don't think he should be allowed to go out any more tonight, Sam," she said. For a few moments they looked at each other over the boy's head then his father repeated: "Yew can take Floss for a walk. But yew keep outer mischief an' git back hoom afore nine or I'll come arter yew with a stick." His mother turned and went in without another word.

Freddy released the dog chain and the old dog came forth, stiff and mangy from her close quarters in the kennel, hardly believing her luck, trying to remember how to be playful. Freddy pulled a hazel wand from the hedge near the gate and went off down the lane. He dug his toes in the loose sand and thwacked at the hedges, ecstatic with freedom and idleness and wealth. When he came to Beatty's farm and the orchard beside the lane, he walked circumspectly, seeming to be absorbed in his dog. Just the same, he noticed that the apple tree just over the hedge was laden with fruit that had not yet been picked and that the farm was still and quiet. For whoever lived there the day had been worked out, in field and cowshed and barn; now there was nothing more but to wait for tomorrow.

Just beyond the farm, where the lane dwindled to a track that led only to the churchyard and the river, a small figure came into Freddy's view — a diminutive, dawdling shadow ahead of the evening sun. It was Sandy, of course. Sandy had been fishing again.

"Yew catch anything?" asked Freddy as soon as he was within shouting distance. The solitary, fair-haired mite came up slowly and shook his head. "Not yet," he said. He showed his empty jam-jar, the pole with the bent pin at the end of a piece of string and the huge bag that he carried in case he caught something really massive. So far he had not caught anything of an average size or even, to be honest, anything minutely small but the

4

hope and confidence that he would one day succeed was something that filled all his dreams. "I nearly got a big one," he told Freddy.

Freddy retraced his steps with Sandy as far as the orchard, unable to forgo the temptation now that support had arrived. The orchard and the farmhouse behind still slumbered in the evening peace. Opposite the tree that Freddy had marked, he suddenly crouched down and hissed to the startled Sandy: "Howd Floss here for a minute an' keep a look-out — I'm goin' to git a few apples. Lend me yar bag."

Scared and less than half willing but finding it too late to protest, Sandy found himself acting as a look-out man and dog-handler as Freddy disappeared through a hole at the bottom of the orchard hedge. He crept along the ditch for a few yards then through the long grass without disturbing more than the old billy-goat, who threw up his head and looked sagely on as Freddy mounted to the fork of the tree. In frantic haste he tore off apples and put them in the bag, and since the opportunity was too good to miss, pulled out his woollen guernsey like an apron and filled that too.

Hampered with such vast spoils, the getting down from the tree proved more difficult than Freddy had foreseen. Moreover, the goat had come up and taken a position immediately below and was looking up with a kind of patriarchal curiosity. For a few moments Freddy clung in indecision to the stout arms of the tree, until he heard sounds of impatience and anxiety from Sandy on the other side of the hedge. He slid down, hurriedly and without grace, scraping his knees and scattering apples all around. The goat sniffed at the apples but found the retreating form of Freddy more interesting and followed

5

after, bleating loudly. A man appeared at the edge of the orchard near the house and shouted as Freddy threw himself through the hole in the hedge and yelled to Sandy to run. Sandy squeaked in terror and ran.

It was an awkward, half-stumbling, panic-stricken retreat. Sandy was cluttered with fishing tackle and jam-jar as well as the heavy bag of apples that Freddy had thrust upon him while Freddy clutched the ungainly load in his sagging guernsey and tried not to leave a trail. Floss was loosed and loped around the pair, hoping it was some kind of game.

"We're runnin' the wrong way," panted Sandy.

"We got to," said Freddy, "we'll work our way back later."

"I should ha' bin hoom," Sandy said reproachfully, "ef yew ha'nt come along."

A fault in Freddy's tactics had got the enemy between them and their homes and there was nothing for it but to run blindly on and into the churchyard. For several minutes, recovering their breath, they hid behind old tombstones that leaned below the yew trees. Now and again they thought they heard footsteps and they peered from behind the stones holding half-eaten apples. Then they began to relax. There was no one coming — there was no one anywhere. The churchyard was so quiet they could hear their own voices beat against the old flint walls of the church tower and come back hollow and lonely. For a time, as the shadows began to grow across the grass and the graves, they lapsed into silence and the only sound came from the munching of apples.

Behind them the two boys began to feel the cool mist as it spread up from the water meadows. Sandy did not fail to notice the first bats swooping above their heads

6

from the church tower. Sandy said: "I want to be a-goin' hoom." Freddy threw an apple he had barely bitten into to lie in the long grass. "We'll atter hide the rest," he told Sandy. "Cos we gotter go back the same way an' we mustn't carry any case they stop us. We can easy git 'em agin another day."

They selected patches of soil where it looked soft to dig and began to scoop the earth away, side by side. Floss, delighted that such a sensible activity had become suddenly popular, set to work with professional enthusiasm to excavate a few yards away. It took the boys some time to bury all the apples. When they looked round for Floss she was still digging and had plenty to show for her efforts. Ranged about the considerable hole she had made were the unmistakable, eerie shapes of bones. "Cripes", said Freddy.

Sandy gulped and stared. "Cripes," he said.

"Human boons — that's execration, ain't it?" breathed Freddy. "Ain't that what it is?"

"Dessication, yew mean," Sandy whispered. "A-touchin' o' holy things — that's dessication."

"Well, we din't touch 'em did we? Arter all, Floss don't know no better. Sandy, d'yew really think them boons are holy?"

"Yeah, ef they're peoples' boons they're holy." They were talking almost in whispers. "We'd be holy too ef we was jest boons."

There was a pause and the absurdity of the words struck them both at the same moment and almost split their sides. 'We'd be holy ef we was jest boons," they kept repeating. They rolled about the tombstones, helpless with laughter. Then Freddy ate another apple while Sandy tried to pull Floss away from her excavations and the churchyard suddenly became hushed and gloomy.

"I gotter go hoom," said Sandy.

They picked up the bones and stuffed them into the empty bag quickly — suddenly anxious to get them out of sight and away from the place. When they came into the lane it was quiet and lonely. Moths fluttered in the dusk below the hedges and the trees were very still. When they reached the farm they tip-toed past the darkening orchard but in his acute anxiety to be quiet, Sandy dropped his jam-jar and the shattering noise made them take to their heels again with every kind of imagined horror behind them. Then at last the lane came to an end and it was lighter and they were free.

Freddy's father was there waiting, close to the gate of the cottage. He stood very still and said nothing in greeting and Freddy knew it for a bad sign. He opened the bag and showed his father the bones, explaining hurriedly that they had turned them up when hunting for a rabbit. In the dusk Freddy's father held the bones up near his face, one after another, then felt their shapes before he put them back in the bag.

"Them's sheeps' boons" he said soberly. "They was a lot o' sheep died around here at one time." Freddy tipped the bones out of the bag into the ditch. "I better go in," he said, with placating innocence, 'I 'spect that's nearly nine o'clock."

"There ain't no hurry, boy. Not no more." His father was speaking in a strange low voice and he could barely catch the words. "Your mother ha' gone, Freddy. She ain't there any more. Yew don't atter hurry."

They stood and looked at the house and knew it to be a different house, a place in which they were now strangers. Sandy drifted away, feeling that something weird

8

had happened. "I'm goin' hoom," he said and turned his small, tired legs toward his own home. Suddenly afraid of the loneliness ahead, Freddy called out: "Yew a-comin' out tomorrer, Sandy?" But the gloom had swallowed Sandy up. It was not until he reached the door of his own house that his thin, high voice came back: "Tomorrer I'm goin' fishin'."

Freddy looked at the house dark against the sky and was afraid to enter the black loneliness. He put his arms about the familiar gatepost and cried. His father would have put his arm round him to lead him in but the boy shrank away.

"Yew — silly — sod," he felt himself say, but the words were lost in the sniffs and sobs of his grief and no one heard. "Yew — silly — grut — sod."

Autumn Winds

"Come Michaelmas," we used to say, "there'll be changes." And, come Michaelmas, there always were. They shuffled through the farming community in those unstable times like the autumn wind in loose straw. It was the seasonal end and beginning, the time for settling up or for settling down, for strange new faces to take the places of familiar old ones, for human disturbances amid the calm of mellow fruitfulness. It was the crucible of all our humble affairs — for once Michaelmas was gone the die was cast for another year.

In those days, lives and land were more closely intermingled. For one thing, there were hundreds of families committed to working tiny holdings, some of only a few acres. For such people, Michaelmas was the testing-point, the annual moment of truth. In my childhood the process had already begun of absorbing such small areas of land into larger units and I remember the unhappy experience of witnessing how, one after another, hard-working neighbours gave up and left. First went those who had the greatest disadvantages — land that was poor and hungry or lacking a water supply, or where a man's strength, which was his only capital, was failing. For a time new and optimistic tenants would come along and hang on to the holding with dour determination but the tenancies were for shorter and shorter periods. Finally the place would be taken up, absorbed into a neighbouring farm and disappear as a separate entity with no sign to record the years of labour that had been wrought upon it.

Giving up land on which he had sweated to maintain his family, as well as his own pride and independence, was a hard thing for a man to do, I remember how old Hoppy Mayes, who was a neighbour of ours, came face to face with his last Michaelmas that year that he lost the battle. He trudged along the lane to our back door one fine September day, old and bent like the stale of a scythe and with hands claw-shaped with incessant use. We had never before seen him when he was not engaged in some task or driving his cart to market; it was a shock to see him at our door as if he were disarmed and lost.

My father had just finished his meal and he came to the door when we told him who was there. Hoppy, who had one leg slightly shorter than the other and consequently a limp, stood on the boot-scraper outside and tried to put some heartiness into his woe-begone expression.

"George," he said with his old-fashioned directness, "that ain't the fust toime I bin ter ask yew fer a helpin' hand. Still, yew ain't ever refused me yit an' haps this'll be the last toime I s'll atter ask. Thing is, I'll be wholly glad o' the loan o' yar hoss an' cart for a couple o' hours, owd pardner."

"Yew want ter come in?" asked father hospitably.

"No, thank ye kindly. I ha'n't ought ter trouble yew at all — but yew know how I'm sittevated. That ain't no good me hangin' on no longer — can't git blood out of a stoon. See, I got the sale Monday an' I a'riddy sowd my owd mare."

"I'll gi'e ye a hand," my father said.

"No need, owd pardner," Hoppy said cheerfully. But father was not to be put off. His insistence was not entirely on humanitarian grounds — though he was more ready than most to help a lame dog over a stile — and to pretend that it was would be giving a false picture of those days when shrewd opportunism was the only weapon to ward off defeat. There could be something around the holding that he wanted and might be going cheap or even for the asking seeing he was lending the horse.

Father harnessed Jack straight away to the farm cart and the two men set themselves stiffly on the board seat side by side while two or three of us children, always on hand when something interesting was happening, climbed into the back.

"I thought yew might be a-givin' up tew," Hoppy was saying to father, "yew with yar big family — all them mouths ter feed." Father reached for the whip to touch the horse and his face was grim as he answered: "No, not yit — not quite yit, Hoppy."

That afternoon was spent happily enough by us children, no matter that it was something quite different for our elders. We watched Hoppy and his wife carting out the clutter of objects from sheds and pig-sties and spreading them out for sale. The few head of stock had already gone except for a couple of goats and a litter of pigs with the sow. The rest consisted of a few basic implements, hand-tools and utensils, a small stack of hay and a handful of stover. When Hoppy had cleared the buildings of everything that might fetch a few pence, he began to drag the furniture from the house. When the day of the sale arrived, neighbours would come with horses and carts and take away loads of rubbish, old timber and harness, oil lamps and kitchen furniture, pig troughs and wire-netting and add them to their own poor stock of

12

worldly goods.

So far as we youngsters were concerned, there was a great deal on the holding of more immediate interest and value, though it was worth nothing in cash. There was the inevitable orchard, for example, with apple and pear trees of ancient lineage and prodigious height, dropping its harvest into the long grass for the wasps and mice to share. There were a couple of prized damson and a walnut tree and in the rough hedge-rows the bullaces hung like grapes from half-forgotten trees. In such things, and for young boys, Michaelmas was a good time to know and still remains a good time to remember, with the taste and smell and contentment of autumn in the air. That year the sun was warm and mellow, burnishing one lazy day after another in a kinder, Indian summer. In this pleasant mood of repletion the earth rested while mere humans made their desperate Michaelmas reckonings on survival.

"Any rate," old Hoppy chuckled with grim satisfaction, "I shall know now how I stand." He had brought out an armful of utensils from the house and put them down where father was examining a heap of old harness for a likely bridle. Hoppy stayed for a moment looking across the fields, the lines of fifty years of labour imprinted in his face. "Never knew that afore," he said softly, recalling the years. "Never hev known, one harvest ter the next —"

Father nodded in understanding. Not knowing how one stood was always part of the burden — the endless uncertainties of prices and of weather and of crops that made a man unwilling to commit himself to more than the most stringent outlay for the future — till Michaelmas came round again and he had to decide whether he

13

should sell up or struggle on for another year.

"How much?" my father asked Hoppy. He indicated a bridle with reins, a rat-eaten meal bin and a small collection of odds and ends. It was a formal question and indicated that father thought it a fair swop for borrowing his horse and cart. Whatever the circumstances, each day had to show some small gain or we would go the way of Hoppy Mayes and his family. "Yo're very welcome," Hoppy agreed in his courteous way.

The day following the sale, Father drove the cart once again over to Hoppy Mayes' holding for the last time. He was to take them to the station, a journey he hoped would be paid for by picking up some forgotten trifles on the holding on the way back. Hoppy was waiting by his empty house looking strangely parcelled up in a new jacket and a celluloid collar. There was not enough room on the seat for his wife and she clambered heavily into the back of the cart and sat on a bag of straw.

"We're a-goin' ter har sister's," Hoppy told Father. "She live in Leicester — wherever that may be. She say she got room enough an' glad o' the company."

"Sisters-in-law ain't much cop as a rule," my father said. The old man slowly nodded his head in agreement.

"Got ter go somewhere," he said. "At least that ain't the wukkus."

"Yew should ha' stayed," said Father.

"Well, tha's done now, owd pardner. Yew forgit I ain't gittin' any younger."

"Yew 'on't git any younger along o' yar sister-in-law either," pointed out my father bluntly.

The old man twisted in his uncomfortable collar to look sadly at the passing fields. "No, I don't reckon that'll last me long," he said quietly. "On me own, I'd ha' stuck

out, come what may. But I atter think o' the missus —
she ain't had a lotter comfort these few years, poor owd
dear."

At the station the couple stood awkwardly by the
wicker basket that contained all that they had left of
worldy possessions. Hoppy stood on his unequal legs
and stared at the basket and at his missus and at the
station-master in his gold-braid cap. All the time he held
his hands stiff as if he were grasping an invisible tool and
his head was bent as if he were fighting with the soil still,
as he would wherever he went, for the rest of life.

Father whipped up the horse as we left the station. At
Hoppy's empty holding, just before sunset, we filled the
cart with hay, tiles, planks, a peck of apples and one or
two other things that Father had put away out of sight.

Darkie Ward

Darkie Ward always had a story to tell. Darkie would stump into town every so often from whatever mysterious backwater he lived in, straight down the middle of the road with his thumb-stick adding its regular tapping in accompaniment to the clatter of his hob-nail boots — and he would be hungry for someone to listen to him.

Listen we would, though it was an accepted fact that you could not believe half of what he said. The thing was that all of Darkie's unlikely tales were woven into the familiar countryside about us. He conjured magic and excitement from dull village life and invested it in characters of whom we have never seen the like. To our everlasting amusement he always talked in a high, wandering kind of voice that sometimes broke into a falsetto and made the narrative seem a sort of hilarious comment on a staid world. He was a character removed from the unimaginative details of practical reality, abstracted yet anxious that others should join in his dreams.

One day each year when Darkie could be sure to have an audience was on Easter Monday when he unfailingly turned up at the Woodbridge Horse Show. In those days the show used to be held on the Fen Meadow and the streets seemed to be full of country folk and of majestic Suffolk Punches coming from the station, a sight to wonder at as they shied and sidled in glossy magnificence through the crowds.

On this particular Easter Monday the weather was a mixture of sun and showers and before the end of the afternoon the stallions on the showground steamed and snorted in their hessian cubicles as mere dwarfs of men anxiously rubbed them down and replaited their manes.

During one wet spell Darkie joined a group of people sheltering in a corner of a marquee and before long was holding forth to his captive audience. As I remember it, it was a tale only slightly tinged with Darkie's fantasies and for once seemed to have the touch of truth.

"Years ago (said Darkie) I used to go hoom from wark along of a narrer lane what was a short cut. Them days I was handyman an' coochman an' Lord know what up at the Rectory."

He broke off for a moment as if wondering at his own strange history, then went on: "One day I was a-walkin' along this here lane an' I see a little owd eye a-lookin' at me out o' the hedge. Well, course that wor'n't no eye, but no matter — that was suffen a-glintin' an' a-shimmerin' in the leaves."

"Fust time I thought well blow me ef that ain't a glow-worm. I ain't sin one o' them for years. Then I took ut ter be an owd tin or a bit o' glass but I di'n't trouble ter find out till I went past agin later in the day."

"Funny thing how that happened. 'Stid o' goin' past I stopped at that there spot where that little owd eye was a-winkin' an' I went an' had a look over the hedge. I could see what that was, then; that was a button. That was jist a shiny sort o' button — on'y thing was that was still on a coat an' the coat was still on the bloke what owned ut. Yew could see that was a body — same as someone covered up in a bed, the same shape like."

"Course, I could see hew that was in a minute. That

17

worn't no mystery ter me — that was owd Bob Coates. He lay there in his coat 'cause he cou'n't move an' he cou'n't move cause he was dead — well, he fare ter be, anyway. Poor owd Bob, he lay there an' he di'n't move a muscle. I did. I was off down that rood like hell-for-leather. 'That's owd Bob Coates,' I say ter the sergeant at the police station. 'That's owd Bob Coates an' no mistake, an' he's a-lyin' there dead.'"

"'Ef that is,' say the sergeant, 'tha's under very strange circumstances. Owd Bob ain't bin out o' his cottage fer the last tew year. I ha' knowed Bob half me life an' he ain't ever done this sort o' thing afore. What ever was owd Sarah a-thinkin' of — lettin' him go out?'"

"Well, orf he go, the sergeant, on his bike an' I foller on behind 'cause in a manner o' speakin' that was my body an' I showed him the exact spot where that was. Shore enough, the owd man was dead — but jest a-lying' there comfortable as if he was a-hevin' a nap."

"The sergeant, he kep' puzzlin' over this. Then he say 'we better go an' see owd Sarah,' he say, 'we better let har know an' see ef she can shed any light on the matter.'"

"Well, the house where Bob an' Sarah lived, that was out o' the village abit, on the edge of a wood. Bob bein' a gamekeeper afore he got tew owd, them tew had lived in that cottage for about fifty year. That was a wholly pretty spot an' very quiet. All we could hear when the sergeant an' me got there was these doves in the trees."

"There di'n't fare ter be anybody about so the sergeant he opened the little owd wicket gate an' went up the path an' knocked on the door. 'Look at that there garden, Darkie,' he say ter me. 'J'ever see anything as pretty as that?' Well, we took ter walkin' round the garden while we was waitin' but still no one come ter the door. I c'd see the sergeant was a-gittin' a bit worried about this an' at last he went an' lifted the latch an' went in the cottage an' I follered behind. Blow me, owd Sarah was a-sittin' there at the table. There was one o' them fancy clorths on the table an' the room that looked as clean as a new pin. Owd Sarah was jest a-sittin' there wearin' har best shawl an' apron; she was sittin' right still an' lookin' at the owd Family Bible."

"'Ef yo're come from the Union,' she say without lookin' up, 'you can go back agin. There ain't no one in this house a-goin' ter the work-house,' she say."

"'Tha's me, Sarah', the sergeant say. 'Yew know me — an' this is owd Darkie Ward. I'm afraid we got some bad news for ye, Sarah. We jest now found poor Bob a-lyin' in the spinney there an' I got ter tell yer he's dead.'"

"The owd gal still sat there. She put the pen down she'd bin writin' with in the Bible then she say 'I know,' she say, 'He wanted ter make sure he went fust. He cou'n't bear ter think he might be left behind on his own.'"

"The sergeant he got a bit official. 'Yew better tell me how that happen, Sarah.'"

"'That was his favourite part o' the woods — down there in that spinney.' said Sarah, more as if she was talkin' ter harself than ter us, 'fifty year ago he raised his fust lot o' pheasants aside o' that — afore he got tew old he use ter often walk down there on his own. Y'know, fifty year ain't all that long when yew look back — don't seem but yisterday since we got married, yit the family hev all growed up an' gone. We ain't never bin apart all that time, not me an' Bob, not once in fifty odd years. We was happy tergither.'"

19

"'Trouble is,' she went on, 'times change, people change. This cottage was sold wi' the farm tew year ago an' the new owner he want ut fer one o' his min. That's on'y right — I remember someone had ter move out when we come in all that time ago. On'y we ain't got nowhere else ter go 'cept that place up the hill. We know we cou'n't dew that, not Bob an' me, arter bein' tergither — y'know, they separate ye when yew go in there.'"

"'We never said much about ut', Sarah went on, 'but I knew when he got up this mornin' that was the end. He put on his coat an' he say "I'm a goin' for a walk Sarah", he say. "I'm a-goin' for a walk down the spinney." He ha'n't bin out o' the gate fer tew year but he say "I'm goin' fer a walk, Sarah." I watched him git riddy an' all I say was dew yew want yar stick, Bob? I knew I shou'n't see him alive agin.'"

"'Don't yew git ideas he might ha' committed suicide. He jest went the way he wanted ter go. He was afraid I might go fust. But I waited — I wor'n't riddy ter go afore he did. Now, dew yew bring him back here to this house fer the last time. That 'on't be a pauper funeral 'cause I saved fer that,' she say."

"Sarah came to the door to see us out. She stood in the little porch an' looked an' smelt the summer flowers. "Oh,' she say, 'that candytuft ha' come out at last. Tha's bin a master time comin' inter flower but that look real pretty now.'"

"We went down the path an' the sergeant latched the gate an' looked back at the cottage. 'Goodbye, Sarah,' he say."

"He di'n't speak all the way back ter the village, then he say: 'That was a happy house, Darkie, they had some happy times there when the family was tergither. An' they 'on't ever separate now. She 'on't let him go alone.'"

"An' tha's how that was. They was buried tergither, the same day an' when folk come ter look at the Family Bible what was still open on the cottage table they found she'd already put both their names ter die on the same day."

Family Feud

You could always tell it was Sunday in the days before the 1914—1918 War brought an end to the old-fashioned Sabbath. Sunday was the day when the faint odour of sanctity that had existed in the house all the week burst into sudden fragrance.

Suddenly the purpose and the tone of domestic life changed. Things which had been merely passive all the week, like the best soap which was never to be used for hands that were merely dirty, the blacked boots and the walking stick that waited in the porch as well as the pressed gloves placed ready by the prayer book in the parlour — all now came into service.

There was a reason at last for all the ironing and gophering, the starching and the darning done so patiently on weekdays. Other things, too; the clean smell of lavender bags disturbed in the chests of drawers, rustling dresses, the scrubbed flags of the kitchen floor, the buttonhole posies of garden flowers — and the immense, dragging inactivity. All were important to the Sabbath.

Such long-accustomed ways, accompanied by church bells ang long sermons and an absence of labour had a cathartic effect on village folk. In a single day all priorities were changed and humble families that struggled to exist from Monday to Saturday now sought some kind of blessing and achieved some kind of simple elegance on this separate day.

The only Sunday rebel in our village in those days was

old Ephraim. Twice each Sunday he walked the two miles to attend church services in the next village, thus shunning and shocking the local rector. It was a scandalous liberty to take with social custom. Luckily for him he was an independent tradesman or he might have found himself out of a job.

Close by Ephraim's at the Glebe Cottage there was the Robinson family, where an abundance of children were somehow scrubbed, dressed and restrained to sober Sabbath behaviour, chiefly by threats of physical violence by their parents. The boys found it very hard for on Sunday even the fetching of the skim milk from the farm was denied them. On this day it was the turn of their sister Kitty because she was fifteen and looked so pretty in her wide-sashed dress and long hair and because she would behave with decorum and not bring disgrace on the family.

Kitty was only too pleased to have the privilege. It provided an occasion for being special and self-absorbed; for collecting glances and salutations on the way through the village street and at the end of the journey there was the lovely atmosphere of the farm dairy.

Here, even on summer days, it was always cool and clean with everything filmed with clear water and the milk itself changed from its animal nature to something sweet and water-smelling.

Kitty had some reason for her pride and happiness. She had progressed in her short career at the school from pupil to monitor and now to pupil-teacher. From this stage she hoped to emerge eventually as a fully-fledged uncertificated teacher. Such matters commanded a good deal of respect from the local people and Kitty knew how little they understood of the long hours of work and of the biting criticism that she received from the headmistress and the visiting inspector.

Her status elevated her a little above the labouring families but she retained the basic common sense of her kind, sharing the chores and dropping into the dialect when she was at home. It was unfair to Kitty that she became the unwitting cause of a short but bitter inter-village war.

On this Sunday afternoon Kitty took the milk can from the dresser in the kitchen, looked once more at her hair in the mirror and left the house. Her two brothers, Mick and Sam, 18 and 20 years old, were defying convention and their parents by cleaning their bikes in the garden. As Kitty went past, Sam pushed his bike towards her as if to run over her newly-polished shoes.

"Yew dew," she laughed, "an' I'll brain yew with this can."

"Yew afraid o' a bit o' mud, then?" Sam asked and scooped mud from the mudguard and pretended to chase her. She ran out of the gate, shouting: "Don't forgit my bike need cleaning, tew."

In the village street one or two people who were out admiring their front gardens spoke to her and a woman at the end cottage who was energetically brushing a small boy's hair outside the front door waved in a kindly way.

It was this woman who, when Kitty did not reappear from the lane at her usual time, walked a little way along, in curiosity to find what had detained her. She found Kitty in a cart-shed, sobbing, her dress torn and her hair bedraggled. Dreading the worst, the woman helped Kitty back to her own house and in full sight of the neighbours, took her in.

There followed a quiet but considerable tremor throughout the village. In muted Sunday fashion, excitement and indignation passed like an electric current from house to house until it sparked into activity at the Robinson's. The elder Robinsons appeared and walked properly but quickly to the end cottage where Kitty was recovering.

Mick and Sam went ahead on their bikes, took one look at their sister's dishevelled state, came to their own conclusions and set off up the lane. They found the can, the spilt milk and a piece of muslin caught in the briars. Worse — for everyone in the end — they saw a group of youths in the fields that lay between this and the next village. They were walking along the hedgerows shooting at birds with their catapults. It was the easily recognisable Hawkins boys, whose loutishness was a by-word for miles.

Such tension there was that day and such a need among the younger people for excitement that Mick and Sam had only to whisper the name of Hawkins to be surrounded by a growing army of friends eager for revenge. A selected band obtained sacks and string, catapults and rope and just before five o'clock when the Hawkins could be expected to be sitting down to tea, the Robinsons and their cohorts of hangers-on set off on their bikes intent on retribution.

Sam would have called at the end cottage first to discover what had actually happened to Kitty but was swept on by the mob haste of his companions. It was a pity, since inside the cottage Kitty had soon become her old cheerful self and the general alarm was giving way to relief and smiles. Kitty, who had not even seen the Hawkins boys, was describing how the farm bull, escaped from its box, had chased her down half the length of the lane. She had tried to jump the ditch in a panic but landed painfully in the blackthorn and briar, while the bull passed without interest and wandered into a field.

What with the fright, the humiliation and disappointment at ruining her Sunday dress and losing the milk, she took it all rather badly until her good humour returned. The cottagers who had crowded in took the news resignedly. No excitement after all, really. But Mr. Robinson was looking round in concern. "Where are them tew boys? I'll whelp them dew they git into trouble."

It was at about that moment, in fact, when the large Hawkins family realised that there was a war on. They were sitting peacefully at tea in the kitchen when the fire, which had just provided them all with good thick toast, suddenly belched out and smoke poured from the chimney into the room.

The senior Hawkins, who had some little experience of rural vendettas, shouted: "Look out, togither. Someone ha' put a bag over the chimney. Yew git out there quick afore they git down."

The Hawkins boys charged to the door but found it was tied fast. When they climbed out of the window they were greeted by a hail of stones from catapults and they retreated inside, though not before they had learned who their assailants were.

It was the first of a number of skirmishes between the two families. Usually they were confined to the weekends, whenever a small band could be raised to carry out a raid and provided it did not outrage the Sunday conventions. There were a few broken windows and a collection of bruises on both sides before the campaign ended.

The odd thing was that once the feud started it did not seem to matter in the least how it began or that it had all been caused by a misunderstanding.

Charlie Payne

Every Friday we used to go to the mill with a tumbril for a load of middlings and bran. On a breezy day the sails would be clacking round briskly and the miller would great us from the grinding floor with his head and shoulders covered in a meal sack folded inside itself to make a kind of hood.

Another voluminous sack would be tied round his middle and the whole effect was to give him a distinctly conical shape, as if he had borrowed the idea from the mill itself. We used to say that he needed only another pair of arms to become fully operational!

Although he was always busy in the mill, the miller was a man of substance and of some social standing in the area. He could look as floury and conical as he liked; no one would think of addressing him as anything but Mr. Granby or of indicating that he was not held in the highest esteem and respect.

A similar attitude could never be used towards his nearest neighbour, a disreputable old man who occupied — rather than worked — the piece of land adjacent. This was Charlie Payne, the butt of many of our childish jokes and jeers. As likely as not, we would catch sight of Charlie whenever we visited the mill.

One thing was certain — if Charlie was there, his grey mare would be there too, for they were seldom seen apart and hardly ever when he was not be-rating the poor animal. Of the two, the horse, aged and bony-ribbed as it was, had the balance of dignity for Charlie was humanity at its most basic. The impression was that, whereas the miller earned his living, Charlie fought and schemed and scratched for his.

When I knew him in the early years of the twenties, his desperately hard life had left him hating and distrusting anything that did not bring food to his mouth. He always had a stubble of grey beard and never a shred of civilised behaviour. He scraped along by dealing in old iron, by doing a few odd jobs of carting and by keeping a good number of squealing, under-fed pigs on his piece of land.

The small field he owned was generally growing a bit of lucerne or clover in so far as it was possible between the heaps of old iron and the ramshackle pig-sties and it seemed doubtful if his old horse ever had much more food than was provided in this way.

Apart from his notorious neglect of his horse, Charlie had other dubious reputations — as an outstanding sharp-dealer and as head of a family of legendary proportions. The local quip, which had little humour but a good deal of outraged criticism in it, was that Charlie's wife had had twenty-two children twice over, that is, twenty-three altogether, for the twenty-second child had died and another was born afterwards. This may have been so but I can remember only four sons, who were then grown up but still in awe of their father's authority.

One of them used to make pop-guns from elder wood for a penny each. In the pop-gun season, which was when acorns were plentiful, we would go to the tiny house where the family lived and on more than one occasion met one or other of the sons making a hurried exit, assisted on the way by Charlie's boot.

If it was George, the pop-gun maker, who was leaving home suddenly, you would have to postpone your purchase for a day or two by which time George would be re-instated and another son would be in disgrace.

The miller observed a good deal of the activities of Charlie and his family with disapproving interest. Charlie's reputation and proximity to the mill was one thing that disturbed him but it must be added, in deference to his humanity, that almost equally was he worried by Charlie's maltreatment of his animals, particularly the visibly under-fed grey mare.

As a man of conscience he was aware that he could have provided the horse with an occasional peck of poor-grade oats without being very much out of pocket but at the same time he was chary of giving someone an inch who would almost certainly take a yard.

His few encounters with Charlie Payne had been sin-gularly unprofitable for him — but not for Charlie . On one occasion he had felt moved to remonstrate with Charlie on the fact that his horse had run away twice within a week, putting it down to out-right cruelty, but had ended up by replacing some of the broken harness from his own stable.

At another time he had been careless enough to remark: "Why on earth don't you get the poor beast properly shod?" And Charlie, who had long ago seen the potential profits in the miller's 'softness' had touched his forehead and muttered that he would get it done the very next day.

"An' thank ye kindly, master," he added. The horse was forthwith provided with the unusual treat of a com-plete set of new shoes and much later the miller found that it had been added to the farrier's bill for his own horses. Remembering the words he had used and Char-lie's thanks, he had to admit that it could appear to be a genuine misapprehension. He said no more about it.

Despite his vigilance, the miller could seldom find anything amiss with Charlie's behaviour in other ways. He never crossed the boundary into the mill yard and neither begged nor borrowed tools or grain. Feeling that he might have been unfair in his suspicions, the miller eventually offered Charlie a few days work in clearing the rubbish that had accumulated around the mill.

Among other things there was a considerable heap of sweepings from the mill floor consisting mostly of barley avils and dusty chaff. With little room to dispose of it in the mill yard, Charlie offered to take the refuse back to his side of the fence and burn it there on his land.

From then on he carried a large sack full of the rubbish each time he left off work and tipped it out into a heap. Fearing that this might be a cover for carrying out some grain, the miller always watched Charlie closely, sometimes examining the contents of the sack and looking on when Charlie emptied it.

Charlie, for his part, anxious to prove that there was nothing in the sack but rubbish, would shake it out carefully in full view. The miller was persuaded by such palpable innocence to thank him for getting rid of the rubbish. "I don't mind how much I dew for a good master," Charlie assured him.

At the end of the job the miller gave him half-a-crown extra for a good job and to ease his own conscience. Charlie set fire to the heap of rubbish and chuckled to himself. Next day he took a cart-load of large meal sacks in which he had carried the rubbish and sold them to the miller in the next village.

De Dion Bouton

The De Dion that we acquired in 1925 seemed to have spent itself coming the whole mile and a half from Captain Greaves' place, because it barely wheezed into the yard and then subsided with a fearful clanking noise, looking as if it would never move again. We pushed it aside, since we had a more functional Model T Ford for everyday requirements and saw the De Dion as something that might come in useful to take Mother out on Sunday afternoons.

But somehow that car took a lot of getting used to, even when it was doing nothing but sulking in a corner, because of its brassy affectation and high, throne-like seats. My father had paid ten pounds for the car after the gallant captain moved on to the luxury of an Austin Ten and we were conscious that more progressive people were buying the new bull-nosed Morris with its smart, modern appearance and better performance.

In those days, as now, it was excusable to own something very old or very new but never something just out of date. So we despised the old car as much as it seemed to despise us and in this impasse of dislike the De Dion was neglected for several weeks. Then some attention came from younger members of the family who used it to learn to drive, which in those days meant simply to get the wheels turning. All else was academic which you could pick up as you drove along.

"Can you drive?" my father asked me one day in the middle of dinner. There were ten of us altogether in our family and for the lowest but one to be addressed at all from the head of the table was like winning a mystery prize when you least expected it. In fact, my brothers could drive but I had no trust in nor affection for things mechanical — no, I admitted, I couldn't drive.

"Well, you'd better learn fast," my father said, "because I want you to take your mother to Norwich at three o'clock. That'll get you there in time for tea. Start hoom about eight o'clock an' you'll be back afore lightin' up."

I pointed out my disadvantage and nominated several much more suitable candidates from among my brothers but all, unfortunately, were committed to other activities. The mystery prize turned out to be a handful of dust. I went miserably into the yard and exchanged looks of loathing with the old De Dion. Somehow, however, my brothers coaxed it into life and I found that certain movements with levers and pedals would actually cause it to move.

Father came out with Mother dressed in her best just before three o'clock. "All right?" he said. A negative was unthinkable — if father said "All right?" then it had better be all right. I nodded, shot the car to within an inch of the poultry shed and reversed with less luck to demolish the water butt that had long stood at the corner of the house.

"Go stiddy," said Father equably, seeing it as part of the usual incidents on one's first journey. "You'll sune get used to it".

Mother climbed up beside me and held her hat, since we were open to the wind and weather. "It's lovely fresh air," she told everyone, "I shall enjoy this." There was something in her voice more hopeful than confident but Father cheered us up by advising a complicated route

33

which neither of us could follow and finishing with: "That can't be more'n thutty mile each way."

There was no opportunity to express my belief that I would be as likely to drive sixty miles in that machine as to go round the world. We swung out of the gate at a good pace since I knew only one speed and one gear — until I found another, almost by accident. It was something that made little difference anyway. The De Dion trundled on at an unsteady ten miles an hour no matter what was done by way of encouragement. On the other hand, it was inclined to suffer a kind of genteel vertigo at the prospect of climbing the gentlest slope and invariably came to rest halfway up.

The alternatives then were to back down again and have another attempt at a wild 15 m.p.h., or to get some help to push it to the top where it would recover sufficiently to resume its former break-neck speed.

There were momentary alarms when the spring fell off the accelerator, when the car took to making weaving and waltzing movements because one or two tyres needed pumping up, when a new, bumping noise started in the engine and when Mother forgot to hold her hat and lost it over a hedge. In one village a flock of sheep seemed to be in permanent occupation of the road and the monster was brought to a standstill where it steamed and sulked and took no notice of the turning handle until it was well and cool again.

In those days the roads were shared fairly evenly by motor cars and by horse-drawn vehicles but the sympathy of the rural populace was unmistakeably with the latter and with animals generally. The deeper one went into the country the more baleful and unwelcoming the stares of the disturbed villagers and at one point when I

34

took a wrong turning and we found ourselves in a stack-yard in the midst of rapidly disappearing hens and goats, an irate figure appeared waving a pitch-fork. The stack-yard was large enough for the De Dion to continue in a wide circle and so retreat. Had it come to a stop the signs were that the encounter would not have been a happy one.

Miraculously, we arrived at our destination and later set off for home. A pair of cyclists were waving their arms. "They don't like to be overtaken," I said. Mother nudged my arm.

"Someone's lost a wheel,' she said. One of our tyres was bowling alongside, engaged in a lunatic race with the car. By the time we got home at half past eleven we were on the rims of two wheels, the candles had gone out in the lamps and the old car was jerking and steaming and wheezing like a locomotive. It was already dead, I thought, coming down the last few hundred yards of the road. My brothers came and pushed it into the yard where it refused ever to move again. Only Mother was sorry. "Cars don't have class any more," she said.

The Last Swimming

It was the last swimming in East Anglia, some say the last in the whole of England and it concerned a little old man named Eli Spencer. Eli was nearly seventy, thin and small and, so far as it seems in these more enlightened times, completely harmless and inoffensive. He earned a living in and about the village that betrayed him as a huckster, dealing in any odds and ends on which he could make a few pence profit. The village itself, steeped in the superstitions and ignorance that once characterised the countryside, happened to be well equipped for dealing with wizards and witches, having an immense pond situated in its centre.

Close by old Eli's cottage lived Thomas Bates, who was a thatcher — a master craftsman and a much more respected member of the community. It was Thomas's misfortune to have a wife who was an imbecile. How it came to be that he married such a wife is not clear but to Thomas it was a cross which he felt unable to bear without seeking out some evil cause for the affliction.

On the edge of the parish lived another influential villager, a farmer who sympathised with Thomas Bates and his unjust burden because he himself felt a victim of unnatural powers to the extent that he sometimes seemed to lose his reason. It was expedient for the two men to find a cause for their troubles on which they could lay the full blame and very soon they concluded that there was someone in the village with an evil eye.

It is not hard to imagine the reasons that led to fingers

being pointed to Eli Spencer. After all, he was neither farmer nor worker nor tradesman and he lived alone without wife or family. There was no social group or relative or friend to defend him. People got to staring at Eli whenever they saw his horse and cart and recalling all the bits of gossip they had heard. Some women began to link the huckster with their own misfortunes — whenever he went by, they complained, the butter would not make, the cream would not come. And a shoemaker who had a stall near the green swore that his wax was spoiled whenever Eli was near.

However, it seemed to the elders of the village that more evidence was needed than mere gossip to impugn the old man with witchery. Accordingly, a local farmer was deputed to seek the advice of Billy Abinger, a well-known 'cunning-man' who lived in considerable style from the fees he charged for the powers of second sight. For this consultation with the farmer he received an amount of money that would have paid a man's wages for a month.

There was no doubt, Billy told the farmer, probably divining the answer he wanted if nothing else, that there was an evil agency in the village. So many troubles and upsets came from an unnatural influence that almost certainly originated with Eli Spencer.

From then on, Eli became the object of all the spite that attended the fear of the supernatural. Some fled from his vicinity lest he put the evil eye upon them but others attacked his home and his goods. In despair, he volunteered to submit to the ancient trial of sink or swim.

It was an offer speedily accepted by the village elders, since it absolved them from having to force the test upon Eli and also saved trouble with the clergyman whom then knew to be strongly against such primitive rituals. The event would take place on the Green at the great pond on the following Saturday so that all could see that the trial was properly set out. Four chosen men were to go into the water with Eli, acting as stewards and the constable was to be present to make sure that the swimming was fair and square.

When the day arrived, a large crowd of rural folk assembled and watched the old man in his breeches and shirt wade out into the pond. He was followed by the four men who lifted him bodily and laid him flat on his back on the water. He kept still and floated there for about ten minutes. It was not enough for the crowd of onlookers. Having watched so far in silence they began to feel that it was not the sort of trial they had hoped for. Voices shouted impatiently that he should be tried again.

A second trial brought the same result. The crowd was not satisfied. A man who merely floated was neither sinking nor rising in the water — he would have to be immersed.

"Dip him under," several voices advised. The four stewards standing beside Eli pushed his chest, his feet, his head down. Whatever part they pushed down he still remained buoyant.

The loudest of the critics wanted to go into the pond to make sure Eli was immersed, others blamed the stewards for not trying hard enough. For a few minutes there was an impasse during which the comments and grumbles from the crowd increased and Eli floated on. Then someone suggested that another man of Eli's size and weight should be chosen and that the two should be swum together. Any deviation in Eli's performance from that of the other man would indicate his guilt.

"George Brand — ah, George, he's the one," several agreed. George was brought forward and proved to be of very similar stature to Eli's and thereupon persuaded to return on the following Saturday to share the swim. As for poor Eli, he too promised to come back, being only anxious to get the whole thing over and done with.

News of the primitive trial, however, had reached the Rectory by this time and the following Saturday saw a confrontation between village and parson such as had never been seen before. On that afternoon the crowds had flocked to the pond again and Eli and George were reduced to their shirts and breeches to await the constable as umpire. That worthy was late and the spectators became restive, suspecting that something had gone wrong.

Sure enough, just as the crowd was demanding action, the constable appeared. He was accompanied by the Rector and a churchwarden and there was a sudden silence as the Rector came to the edge of the pond and addressed the villagers.

"There will be no more swimming," he said. "While I have the strength and the power to prevent it there will be no more swimming in this village. Go home, ponder on your own sins. Go home and forget this disgraceful affair."

For a moment the wild element in the crowd looked ready to oppose the Rector. Then, as the women and children moved away, they followed: at the end was old Eli, the last of those poor wretches once tried by swimming.

Ghost in the Garden

I forget what it was that took me to see old Ben Collis on that wild night just before last Christmas. Perhaps it was only because, being fellow villagers for over a generation, we sometimes shared a bottle toward the end of the year and swapped anecdotes of days gone by. But I think now that it was something more positive than chance that took me there on that particular night.

What I do remember, only too clearly, is that there was someone coming from Ben's house when I arrived. Not that I took much notice at the time — it was dark and cold and there was a vicious sleet in the air that kept peoples' heads down and their eyes on the ground. Nevertheless, when I opened the garden gate to go in, a figure was standing there as reasonably clear as one would expect to see in that weather. In fact, he stood aside for a moment — a man, certainly — and I thanked him for his courtesy and went up to the house. I had the impression that he stood there for a few seconds in the darkness, then the gate slammed and he was gone.

It was a minute or two before there was any answer to my knocking. The unlit house and the encounter with the figure at the gate gave me a chilling feeling that all was not right. Then, just as I was about to leave, a light came on, another light — the whole house came to life again — and old Ben was standing in the doorway as hearty and welcoming as ever.

"You've had a visitor already," I remarked, following him to a seat in front of a roaring fire. Old Ben sat down and poked at the logs till the sparks flew, absorbed in the pleasure of warmth and company and I could not be sure that he had heard. At his age he could not be expected to hear and respond to every chance remark. Anyway, it was none of my business and I forgot the matter. We had a game of draughts as was our custom but the game was so drawn out, what with drinking and telling tales, that we often forgot who had moved last. Then the game was over or abandoned and Ben was searching through a box of old photographs.

I could not help noticing, as he brought a handful of the pictures towards the firelight, that he had changed a good deal since I had seen him a year before, a change not only in appearance but in his behaviour. Perhaps, I thought, it was simply the marks of old age, certainly he seemed more forgetful, so distant sometimes that he had to rouse himself to come back to the present.

"Tha's some whoile, I can tell ye, since I had a look at these owd things," he was saying. "I allust reckon tha's like raisin' owd ghosts when yew go lookin' up peoples' likenesses o' long ago. But there's someone here I want yew to hev a look at".

He began to shuffle through the photographs then seemed to remember a phrase he had just used. "Do yew believe in ghosts?" he asked suddenly. I would have laughed but for his serious tone and the memory of the sinister-looking figure at the gate. "Produce one and I'll believe in it," I promised him.

"Well, 'haps I will. Now dew yew look at this hare picture. Whew dew that remind yew of?" It was of a wedding couple. It took me a minute or two to recognise that the handsome young bridegroom was Ben himself as a young man.

41

"Well, I never knew —" I began in utter surprise. Ben was saying, in a voice distant with thoughts of the past: "jest look at har face. Ain't she a proper good-lookin' gal?"

"Never knew you were ever married," I finished, staring at the picture.

"Am married," he corrected me. "Poor Bess — she's still alive in one o' them mental hospitals. She 'on't come out no more. She don't even remember me. She know me jest as someone who go an' visit her sometimes an' take little presents. She look forward to them visits — arter all, tha's the only thing she can look forward tew."

Up to now old Ben seemed to have been fighting against tiredness but now a sudden note of urgency made his voice strong and insistent as he pleaded:

"Anything happen ter me — will yew go an' see what yew can dew for the poor owd gal? Jest go an' say hullo, take a bunch o' flowers, anything. Jest so she got somebody — so she don't fare left out." He handed me a scribbled address. "I recken yew'd dew that for me — ef that so happened that way." His voice was so earnest I promised solemnly that I would go regularly to see his wife should his own visits be brought to an end. He seemed immediately to be pacified and his head began to nod again before the warm fire.

But at the back of my mind I was still bothered, not by his request which I was quite happy to agree to but at my own memory of that dark, ominous figure outside and at his earlier, pointed question: "Do you believe in ghosts?"

"What was the name of your visitor?" I asked him; but there was no answer. I thought I must have tired the old man out. Very quietly I collected my hat and coat and was starting towards the door when he roused himself and muttered as if in a sleep — "Don't yew forgit what yew promised."

"I won't," I said, and left him sitting there in the familiar posture with the firelight throwing shadows across his face. I came out of the door into the cold, blustery wind that brought the chimes of midnight in jagged snatches to my ears.

Halfway down the garden path I came to a sudden, startled halt. At the gate was the same dark figure that I had seen before. To what ghostly vigil was this apparition committed? But it was moving now and coming towards me, seemingly immensely tall and powerful — this time it was I who stood rooted to the spot. The figure came nearer and put itself close in front of me. And spoke:

"What are you doing here?" it asked, in a brisk but everyday sort of voice reminiscent of the local constable. "Perhaps you'd like to tell me how it is you're just coming away from that house?"

It took me all of a minute to take in the questions, to come back to the world of ordinary mortals and to realise that in fact this really was the village constable. I could not help noticing that he was almost as startled as I was.

"Phew," I breathed in relief. "Thank heaven you're real. It's all right about my being here — I've been to see old Ben. You know, when I saw you at the gate for the second time I thought I was seeing a ghost."

"I think you were," the constable answered, coming closer to stare into my face, "if you spent the evening in that house."

"I don't understand", I said. "Why were you watching the cottage? Is Ben Collis in any kind of trouble?"

"You could say so," the policeman answered shortly.

"Come and have a look."

With an uneasy feeling in the pit of my stomach, I followed him back to the door I had just left. The cottage looked dark and silent and unwelcoming. "Gone to bed," I surmised, shivering, "and I don't think we should wake him without good reason. Do you mind telling me what you are doing here?"

"Certainly I will," the policeman answered in a low tone. "There's no mystery about why I'm here. I'm keeping an eye on an empty house."

I stared. "But I played draughts with Ben — we had a drink, talked. In fact, he made a particular request that I should visit his wife if he should die."

"There's a lot of questions here that I can't answer," the law admitted soberly. "Perhaps they're the sort that don't have an answer, not a rational one. There may be something in the idea that the spirit is sometimes strong enough to do miracles. I reckon he hung on somehow so he could give you that message to look after his wife. Let's look inside."

It was not the cold that made me shiver as I went into the cottage again. It needed but a glance to see that the room where we had sat was empty, the fire long ago cold — a room where no one lived.

"The old man was killed in a road accident earlier today," the constable said.

Master Thatcher

Every year after the harvest, Billy Freeman came with his brood of hard-bitten youngsters and a mass of equipment to thatch the cornstacks. The corn would have to stay in the stacks till the travelling threshing tackle came round and that might not be for three or four months. As a temporary measure a canvas tilt was sometimes put over the top but most farmers considered it was a proper, workmanlike finish to the harvest to have the stacks efficiently thatched. For this service, Billy spent a month or more going round the farms out Swaffham way and you could make a map of his journeyings from the special sign he left on the finished stacks. It was his pride, as with many thatchers at that time, to decorate each end of the stack ridge with a chosen symbol — in his case a remarkably life-like pheasant in flight.

Perhaps long ago in his youthful apprenticeship he had spent many hours fashioning the decorative motif but now, with long practice, it took but a minute to twist up a few handfuls of straw and tie in just the right places to create the tell-tale signature for all to see.

Billy always appeared during the mellow September period that followed the back-breaking labour of the harvest. By that time the sheaves had been moved perhaps half-a-dozen times by hand but now at least they would stay put until the threshing. With the corn stacked and the harvest bounty in their pockets, the farm men felt secure for once and ready to be in the best of humour towards Billy when he and his retinue arrived.

It would be early in the day, with the dew still on the meadow grass, when Billy's handcart could be heard approaching the appointed stackyard. Not, of course, that Billy gave himself the task of pulling his own cart. That was left for young Tom, the oldest of the sons, who went ahead with the load of thatching tools and broaches. Billy followed behind with suitable professional dignity, helping himself along with the ash stick that was polished with use. Behind came the two younger boys, fooling around as much as they dared, turning off now and again to reach blackberries or rose hips but never more than momentarily out of their father's sight.

As soon as they arrived at a farm Tom would begin to gavel out the long wheat straw that had been set aside for this purpose. The other boys got water from the pond, laid out the broaches and fetched the long stack ladder. As befitted a craftsman of his standing, Billy took little part in the preparations except to issue a sharp word or a quick cuff on a boy's ear and contented himself with assembling his personal tools and having a relaxed word with the farm men.

Not that Billy ever had much to say. Even in an environment in which speech was professedly basic and economic, to say the least, he was known to be 'close'. Perhaps it was because of his taciturnity that he was believed to be a harsh man in the confines of his cottage though no one could ever prove that this was so. Certainly his word was law among his own but this was in accord with the tradition of patriarchal discipline accepted at that time.

On our own farm the thatching was soon finished — a row of three corn stacks stood under the elms by the pond as firm and neat as cottage loaves and the fourth was going well. Billy stood in the bully-hole left by the stackers and worked from there, easily and confidently, as if every single movement had been thought out long ago.

The armfuls of gavelled straw that young Tom kept bringing tirelessly up the ladder was spread out, tapped close and pegged down securely. At the end, Billy made the tell-tale signature of his completed work, more by habit now than anything else. As usual, he left the bully-hole till last, filling it with loose straw and working the thatch over the top.

Curiously, this was the last stack that Billy ever thatched and the last year that the sign of the flying pheasant was seen in the district. Yet, at the moment when he stood back to admire his own work in the stack-yard he seemed to have no inkling of what lay in store. Perhaps, as a good countryman, he should have learned to read the weather signs more closely.

Like many another father, Billy had forgotten how quickly children grow up. Tom was fifteen now, with years of thatching labour already behind him. Other people had noticed how reserved and resentful Tom was becoming of his father's uncompromising strictness and of the indignity of always being regarded as a child while still expected to do the greater part of the work. But Billy went on in the same old way, keeping a tight hold on the family reins, sometimes half aware that he was wrong but not knowing what other course to take. He remembered the standards of his own youth and followed them to counter the slightest sign of rebellion with punitive measures, often taking off his belt to both Tom and the younger boys. In the few words he felt called upon to address to the children he would give what he considered to be a complete justification.

"Yew ha' got to larn, same as I had tew. Trouble is yew fare to git in yar hids yew c'n dew as yew like sune as yew git away from yar mother's apron strings. Well, yew can't. Till sech time as yew c'n tell what's right behaviour an' what ain't, I shall make sure an' larn ye."

That day at the farm Billy walked round the finished stacks and examined them while Tom collected up all the tools, cleared up round the site and prepared to set off with the handcart and the smaller boys. Billy called him back, curtly nodding to a handful of broaches on the ground and said sourly: "Time ain't come yit we c'n afford to throw good broaches away. Put 'em in the barrer."

Perhaps it was Tom's tiredness that made him hesitate in the very act of obeying his father and behave in a way that he had never done before. In Tom's opinion they were not good broaches and best thrown away but he suddenly realised it would be useless to try and explain this to his father. The relationship was to do with power and not co-operation and Tom decided that it must be simple power as his father understood it, to effect any change.

Deliberately, he picked up half-a-dozen of the thin stakes and threw them one at a time at the symbol of his father's authority, the straw pheasant at the end of the stack. His brothers looked on, aghast. "Bugger the broaches," Tom shouted, his fear of the consequences lost in the need for justice.

Billy unbuckled his belt and would have used it but that Tom closed desperately with him, grabbed the belt and threw it to the ground. For him it was no longer a matter of broaches or tiredness but something much

48

more — a fight for self-respect and manhood. If Billy had withstood him he would have fought his own father, not for hate but to attain his freedom. Like so many others of this age and generation he had found that some of the most loving parents in childhood become mere gaolers in adolescence.

"Use that belt agin an' I'll burn every stack yew thatch. Yew remember that," he told his father in a low voice. He walked home alone; the small brothers pulled the cart home in awed silence and old Billy came slowly, far back down the road, gradually aware that he had been overtaken by the inexorable progress of nature.

From then on, Billy and Tom worked side by side on the stacks but it was Tom who led, who secured and made all shipshape — and who, at the end made his own sign clear and unmistakeable for all to see.

Ben's Little Miracle

There was a sprinkling of snow in the morning, thin and soft — but with a promise of more to come and it brought old Ben Somers to his window to look out at the whirling flakes. It was something that always fascinated him, the way each flake settled as if in a predestined place to weave that virgin carpet and it took his mind back to other winters of long ago.

"Tha's a comin' down," he told Daisy, who was elbow-deep in floury mixtures in the earthenware bowl on the kitchen table. "Not much today, 'haps, but to-morrer — that'll be a different tale. Snow on Christmas Day — jest how that used to be."

Daisy sniffed. "That'd take more'n snow to make a Christmas like they used to be," she said shortly.

Daisy always corrected old Ben. She saw it as her wifely duty, having more plain commonsense and less imagination than the old man, to keep him close to the reality of things and her frequent contradictions were only part of her loving care.

"That wasn't the snow," she told him brusquely, "that made Christmas what it was — it was the foolks. They didn't have the luxuries you see nowadays but they had a rare good neighbourly spirit. But now —" she paused, it hardly seemed necessary to point out the contrast with people nowadays for Ben knew it well enough, but after she had put a batch of mince pies in the oven she concluded — "now, people jest fare to be unsociable an'shut the door on theirselves."

50

Old Ben nodded sadly, filling his pipe by the stove. "Like Fred Stevens next door. He ain't satisfied wi' havin' a Christmas tree — he's got tew on 'em, one in front winder an' one in the back, all lit up an' God knows what else. Yit he don't hev a civil word to say to anybody from one week to the next. As for the folk on the other side" — and the couple thought sadly of the way the world had gone.

Ben and Daisy, both pensioned now, lived in the middle of a row of three cottages situated where the farm lane opened on to the expanse of the open Green. Fred Stevens the tractor driver lived on one side with the three children and his wife Betty who seemed never to be able to cope with all the housework or her husband's bad temper or the childrens' wailing needs.

Too often there were raised voices from that side, arguments shouted above the crying of the children and the oldest boy of eleven — Graham — had taken the habit of getting out of the way and going for long walks on his own or with Rachel Watson, the little girl on the other side.

The Watsons were quiet enough; too quiet, Daisy thought, with them always working in the town and neglecting the garden and leaving Rachel on her own for hours at a time. To top all, both the Stevens and the Watsons considered each other very odd indeed and never spoke.

Ben sat in his chair by the window and thought: "that ain't only the Watsons and the Stevens at loggerheads — tha's everybody else tew. Once that jest used to be the gentry against the working class, now everybody is more equal they fight each other. There's the owd village aginst the newcomers, the council houses aginst the private bungalows, the conservationists aginst the farmers an' the young folk aginst everybody."

There was a thump on the door that interrupted Ben's sombre thoughts. Mrs. Stevens was there, looking distracted as usual, pushing her hair back, asking if they had seen young Graham. "He run out," she said, "arter Fred give 'im a bit of a clout."

"On'y a clip o' the ear," said her husband appearing behind her, "he'll git wuss 'n that when he dew come hoom — a-runnin' off like that."

"Well, I've seen 'im," Daisy said in her short, no-nonsense voice. "He went past wi' little Rachel some time ago."

The Stevens disappeared again breathing fire and slaughter and Ben sat and wondered how miracles were made because if he knew he would certainly like to bring a bit of goodwill back to the village.

He sat up suddenly with the glimmering of an idea, so desperate and unlikely that he dared not even tell Daisy what was in his mind.

"I'm jest a-goin' for a walk," he told her. "While the snow's held up for a bit," and Daisy handed him his stick and his scarf and looked at him quizzically but without a word.

Now the first part of the exercise would be easy enough. He knew where Graham usually hid himself from his parents and no doubt the two children would be there together. So they were. When Ben had climbed stiffly up the ladder of the hay-loft in the off-hand farm buildings, he found both of them fast asleep, half covered in hay and surrounded by a litter of potato crisp bags and belongings. It looked as if the children had come determined to spend the day out of the way of their families.

All the better, Ben thought. He quietly picked up a small red hat, a glove and a handkerchief and put them in this pocket.

Back on the Green, the old man stopped at the phone box, and used the unfamiliar contraption to make three local calls to farms situated on the edge of the village. He was careful to ask only the question that had been asked of him — "Hev yew seen young Graham Stevens or Rachel Watson?"

He knew that the question would be in people's minds all over the village within an hour or so and he chuckled as he set off on the second part of the miracle that took him on a long walk that was shrewdly mapped in his mind and did not bring him back to his cottage until noon.

He was tired and Daisy was sharp with him. "Whatever made yew go so far in sich weather — that fare to me yew don't git no wiser as yew git older."

"I was a-castin' bread on the waters," was all he would say and dozed until Daisy put his dinner before him. For another hour a mid-day lethargy settled over the cottage, over the Green and over the whole village. Then the young sons at Birch Farm walked out with guns and almost at once stumbled upon Rachel's little red hat, replaced guns with sticks and began to search along the coppice nearby. A man with a dog found a glove by the stream and a group of children ran along to Heartsease Farm with an initialled handkerchief.

In half an hour a score of people were walking the fields at the end of the village and Captain Phillips from the Hall came screeching into the village in his Land-rover for direct information. He went to see the Watson's but came out immediately, went into Ben's cottage and

53

spread a map of the village on the table.

"Can't hear myself speak, next door," he said. "Now, we don't know if this young pair are really missing but it can't do any harm to get everybody looking, just in case. I'll get the whole village out — if we find 'em so much the better. Anyway, we'll search around for a couple of hours before we tell the police."

Then the captain was gone again with another scream of tyres and Ben was left to imagine what was happening in the fields and lanes, in the woods and in the cottages all around — for this was the important part of the miracle.

At half past three, as the afternoon fell into winter shadows, Ben walked along to the childrens' hiding place in the barn once more and persuaded them without much difficulty to return home, taking them first into his own cottage to thaw out by the kitchen stove and prepare themselves for recriminations. Daisy sent for the two mothers and they came in together, too relieved and tearfully thankful to be angry. Daisy sent them all back after a few minutes with instructions to prepare refreshments and open their cottage doors for the searchers.

Then the captain came racing in again and he was told the good news that the children had been found. "Thank God for that," he said heartily but dropped his eyes for a moment as if half regretful that the campaign was over. The news spread as groups of searchers converged on the Green, cold and tired but exulting at the happy outcome.

Snow was beginning to fall again, thin veils blowing and swirling like mist as the men came in to the warmth of the cottages feeling in buoyant mood. A wealth of food and drink and conviviality awaited them and all those who came crowding in from the darkness. There were those who wanted to continue the friendships discovered during the afternoon search, those who would have liked to talk about Christmases long gone, others who felt the occasion demanded a good seasoning of jolly songs — and all getting their way to some extent in the riot of good-humoured confusion.

There was a cheer when the two children made a shame-faced appearance and then a cheer for the captain and a cheer for something else — it didn't matter much what it was. Ben brought out his long-saved bottle of whiskey.

"Never seen anything like it — not since VE day," the captain told him, shouting above the din. "The funny thing is I reckon the whole thing was a hoax. The way those gloves and things were strewn around — too deliberate — something like an old-vashioned paper chase."

Ben looked round at the hilarious gathering. "Jest suppose," he said quietly, then spoke out loud for the captain to hear; "jest suppose that was on'y a paper chase. Don't yew think tha's worth it?"

The captain looked at him for a minute, then smiled and shot out his hand. "Every bit. You know, some of these people haven't had a smile for months. Yet today they've spent hours outdoors in bitter cold weather looking for kids who were not really lost and they're as happy as sandboys."

"Well, I think I can tell yew why, master," said old Ben. "Tha's cos they had a chance to dew suffen for somebody else, somebody they thought needed help — a chance to give for a change, "stid o' take. Underneath, I reckon tha's what people want more'n anything."

By six o'clock most of the searchers had gone home but many stayed on engrossed in new friendships or old topics. Daisy began to set out her tins for baking again and the two children curled up sleepily on the couch. Mr. Stevens came whisking in and out, bringing one of his Christmas trees and then armfuls of trimmings. Mrs. Watson watched Daisy making sausage-rolls as excitedly as any school girl.

Then the cottage was empty at last. But now there was the sense of echoing laughter and noise and friendship still. Ben sat in his corner and smelled the new baking and the tree and the long-memoried flavour of Christmas. Daisy brought him a hot mince-pie and gave him a kiss on the cheek. "More'n yew deserve," she scolded, "for whatever yew bin up tew. Trouble is, miracles don't last — at least not your sort."

"Somethin' remain," insisted Ben comfortably. "Tha's like the snow — that soon disappear but yew allust remember what it was like. Folk 'll remember today — arter all, that was on'y a little miracle, m'dear."

"Well don't yew set thinkin' about miracles tomorrow. Jest leave them things to the good Lord."

"That I will," agreed Ben, "he's welcome to that job. It's jest that, now an' agin, when things don't seem to be goin' right, yew arter jog his elbow a bit"

Moocher Crane

Those people who can remember Moocher Crane, most notorious of all poachers in this part of the country nearly fifty years ago, will be surprised to know that there was a time in his life when he turned his back on his chosen profession.

Not only that, but he also felt constrained to post upon his front gate a scrawled notice disclaiming all interest in the pursuit of game.

"All them that seek to take away my Good Name shall be sewed," the notice said. And, underneath, to prove his new-found innocence he added: "Gun for Sale, cheap."

In fact, friends and cronies of Moocher were not unduly worried by the reformation or by the sacrifice of the gun, knowing that two more fine pieces stood by the chimney place in the cottage. All the same, they kept a wary eye upon him because they could never tell what kind of trick Moocher would pull next.

Moocher, however, was genuinely disturbed, not because he suddenly felt scruples about his way of life but because he realised that his own fame had temporarily laid him by the heels. A new, young squire had come into the Hall and into possession of the 2000 acres that had been Moocher's happy hunting ground and had let it be known that he intended to keep a firm hand on every pheasant and rabbit on the place.

Worse still, there were two new and unpleasantly conscientious gamekeepers who had sought Moocher out and warned him off. From now on, they told him, they

57

would watch every step he took and if he so much as put a foot on the squire's land, the squire would be only too happy to prosecute him as an example.

It was a challenging, but not a desperate, situation. Certainly he had never before had such a blunt confrontation with the enemy, except on the one or two occasions when he had been caught in the act and that, of course, was fair enough. To be warned off in such uncompromising terms was something that required thinking about. Moocher retired into his cottage that was set so conveniently on the edge of the wooded part of the estate and brooded for a week.

When he came out again into a closely-watching world, it was as a reformed character whose soul was not only white but would be demonstrably purer than snow. The notice on the gate was the first indication but should anyone still doubt his changed attitude he openly threw an armful of traps and snares into the village pond. His innocence, he told himself as he pulled them out again the same night by the thin line attached and hidden in the reeds, must be the first consideration.

So, while gamekeepers watched the cottage and Moocher's activities from the edge of the wood, he pursued the unfamiliar role of saint and meditating recluse, occupying himself with the cottage garden and even taking out the heavy old family Bible to read on the porch and at night he appeared never to stir from his fire and his books.

In fact, this was a time of supreme awareness for Moocher, watching even while he was being watched, learning the very last detail of his adversaries' habits, studying their routines, their dogs and their guns and knowing that, in the end, by desperate will and superior wit, he would win. Nevertheless it was a period of bitter frustration, particularly when he examined all the familiar apparatus of his trade as it lay useless in the shed. There was nothing that he dared use; even his favourite lures and cages of call-birds, his decoys and flirt-sticks had to be discarded, since the vigilance of the enemy was unceasing.

Even more ominous, estate workmen had gone round the whole perimeter of the estate with stout posts and barbed wire above the usual netting so that now, in addition to the hedge that separated Moocher's garden from the woods and their wealth of game there was the inner fence of strong mesh wire. From his Bible-reading position on the porch, Moocher surveyed the fence and the hedge and listened to the tantalising sounds of the wild-life beyond. For a poacher, he thought, he was becoming stiff and fat and too fond of his bed; moreover at this rate he would soon be hungry. It was time he made a move.

He began by spreading the word around in the village that while he himself was patently innocent of any thought of plundering game, there were others on the opposite side of the estate who were making raids and getting off scot-free. Sure enough, a gun had been heard on one or two occasions (from Moocher's friend Joe, keeping well out of sight) and the two gamekeepers had dutifully rush off leaving a very decent interval in which Moocher squeezed through the hedge, loosened the lower staples holding the wire and found it easy to lift the netting out of the leaf-mould and replace it.

He spent a pleasant evening on his side of the hedge, working out of sight. By the time he was finished there were six neat, funnel-shaped holes in the bottom of the hedge no bigger than a teacup but each cunningly encircled by a snare. At dusk he was able to locate the shapes of several pheasants roosting in the trees inside the wood. When the distant gun went off again as arranged, Moocher waited until the gamekeepers had got well away, entered the woods about 200 yards up the lane and beat the trees and bushes back to the fence and the snares.

Before the gamekeepers returned the wire had been replaced and no sign remained of the four cock pheasants captured. Moocher knew that such a manoeuvre had only a limited life. It worked twice more: then on the third occasion that a shot was heard only one keeper went off, the other remaining suspiciously near the cottage. Despite this, Moocher was quite contented. He had breached the enemy's defences and could do so time and time again knowing all the tricks that he did.

On the very next evening, as it became dusk, he walked boldly up the main driveway as far as the gardener's cottage. Palpably innocent and anxious, he told the gardener that he had heard grunting sounds in the wood and thought that some of the pigs must have got out. Sure enough, a sow and a litter of ten pigs were missing and the sty door had apparently never been bolted by the pig-man. Moocher indicated the area, well away from his cottage, where he thought he had heard the pigs and gardener and keepers set out to search while he walked back down the drive, his duty done.

The fact that he systematically beat his way through the woods on his way home and bagged a rabbit, three pheasants as well as two small pigs was only a just reward. Before Moocher could put any other ideas into action he was sent for by the new squire and duly presented himself at the Hall.

"I think," said the squire shrewdly, "it would be better for both of us, Crane, if we were on the same side, don't you?"

Moocher achieved a non-committal answer by touching his forelock.

"The fact is," continued the squire, "that my keepers have to spend a considerable amount of their time in the fruitless task of watching your cottage. I cannot afford to pay gamekeepers to play policemen — there are more important things for them to do. Since you have made it clear that you have changed from your former poaching habits I wonder how you would like to join them as a third game-keeper?"

This was more than Moocher had bargained for. He managed to indicate, by frequent touching of his forelock, that he bore undying loyalty to the squire class but could not so betray his friends.

"Very well, then, it's the pheasants for me and the rabbits for you. Satisfied? Don't forget that a rabbit has four legs, not two."

So Moocher was back in business again. Contentedly he laid his traps for rabbits and prospered. When, as sometimes happened, a pheasant was stupid enough not to recognise that a trap was set exclusively for rabbits and got caught, Moocher was forced to put the bird into his bag. And rather than waste it, he forced himself to eat it for his dinner the next day.

Ned and Lugsy

The man we knew as 'Owd Arterwards' or more usually as Ned was an odd mixture of gipsy and countryman, a character stocky in build and coarse of nature, with a rasping voice that carried easily across the dykes and levels of his native Fens. Had he been as taciturn as his fellow workers on the farm the fact would have mattered little but Ned had the habit of ruminating aloud.

He would straighten his back from some task or other and deliver observations without context or reason to anyone within hailing distance. His favourite remark, from which he derived his nickname, was cautionary of future consequences. "That's owd arterwards," he would pronounce hoarsely. "That ain't now — that's owd arterwards that count." This odd little bit of wisdom seemed to give him considerable satisfaction and to affect his attitude to the future with a kind of canny apprehension.

During the war years when labour was scarce, Ned was roped in for essential work and turned up intermittently on a farm a mile or two from his home to which he had been directed. His extended absences from the farm and the war effort generally were never explained in detail but were widely believed to be related to his earlier interests in such things as poaching, higgling and horse-dealing. Certainly he was unreliable to the extent that the War Ag. Committee felt constrained to send another old-timer to the farm to assist.

The new man was as much of a character as Ned, though in quite a different way. He was an elderly Londoner who had evacuated himself from the blitz, a thin, spare man who in complete contrast to Ned, spoke in a quiet, town-bred way and behaved even in the worst circumstances with determined good manners and Cockney humour. It was something that Ned found very trying on the many occasions when the two men had to work together. He felt that he had had a lot of hard things to put up with since coming to work on the farm but nothing so downright irksome as the Londoner's politeness. More than once when the Londoner (whom Ned called Lugsy because of his reluctance to respond to his cruder remarks) was only offering a courteous helping hand, Ned would stare at him in aggressive indecision as to whether to offer to swipe him forthwith or to be charitable and put it all down to citified softness.

Gradually, however, as the two men worked side by side they developed a kind of guarded respect for each other's separate idiosyncrasies. At elevenses, for example, Lugsy would sit himself primly at the base of a hedge to eat his sandwiches while Ned took his thumb-piece and pocket-knife to squat some twenty yards from the hedge in the open field. Here he covered himself with an assortment of coats and sacks until he looked like a homely Buddha and would then direct a rasping monologue across the intervening space on the dangers of draughts that penetrated hedges and entered the vitals.

At that time, Ned was much absorbed by the question of marriage, especially since what should have been a primrose path to the altar was apparently littered with difficulties. A local widow had entered into some sort of coquettish relationship with him, the purpose and progress of which was probably clear to her but largely perplexing and frustrating to the ingenuous Ned. In this matter he had none of the confidence and expertise that attended his dealings with horses. The saga of his marital hopes and fears was declaimed daily in a voice which no one on the farm could fail to hear.

On some mornings he would turn up in ribald good humour. "She's a rare good-looking' woman, that there widder," he would bellow. "An' she got some rare timber on har — thet she hev." He would look round to include anyone who might be remotely within earshot. "She got some rare timber. That she hev."

On other occasions the material assets potential in the alliance would excite his higgler's nature. "Thet's a bargain, ain't it, Lugsy? Thet widder women, she got a houseful o' furniture an' a proper good bike what her owd man left in the shed. What about thet, Lugsy? A fine widder-woman to keep me warm an' har own furniture an' a bike what's a'most new. Thet's a good bargain, ain't it?"

There were days when he was beset with doubts. He doubted whether the widow would be a loyal wife, whether he could afford to keep such a paragon of virtues and whether, indeed, he really wanted to marry her at all. Eventually he asked Lugsy if he would visit the widow and try to sort out the situation and put it in masculine terms so that he could understand. "That's don't seem I can git any forrader wi' the woman," he complained. This the sociable Lugsy agreed to do, privately believing that Ned's own crudeness and inexperience was the stumbling block. However, it was some days before Lugsy found occasion to visit the widow and it must have been during this time of uncertainty that Ned finally relinquished his desire to marry, though retaining an affection for the furniture and the bike.

Lugsy was only too successful in his mission. From the time when he stood on the doorstep, hat in hand, explaining with the utmost civility the purpose of his visit and even more later when he bought separate packages of fish and chips and showed his good manners in the use of the condiments, the widow was captivated anew. During the next few days the two men eyed each other closely but said nothing. Ned had a shrewd idea of what had happened but for once kept his counsel. In the end, torn by feelings of guilt, Lugsy felt himself forced to confess without much enthusiasm that the widow was now promised to him. He began to make a long apology until Ned, seizing the cue for which he had been waiting, bellowed his protests in a voice that not only drowned Lugsy's words but caused farm-workers in many a lonely field round about to prick up their ears and listen.

"Who'd ha' thought anybody could stab his own mate in the back like you hev? Hev I stabbed you in the back jest cos you was deep in love? All I done wrong was to fall in love very deep with a little widder-woman an' you go behind my back an' take her away. You ha' robbed me, Lugsy — you an' yar lah-de-dah ways."

Lugsy was not unduly put out by the rhetoric, knowing that Ned roared most when least hurt. "She did say," he offered mildly, as soon as he could be heard, "she did say that if you were very upset about it she'd be willing to let you have the bike — in compensation for your hurt feelings."

Ned stared at him with no more than a flicker of triumph. "That's the least she c'd dew," he told Lugsy, "for what I'm a-sufferin' that's the very least she c'd dew."

During the weeks that followed, Ned and Lugsy continued to work equably side by side and the affair of the widow was gradually forgotten, though now and then Ned would straighten his back and give a loud chuckle, thinking of the beautiful bicycle now kept in his own kitchen and he would bellow: "Cor, she had some rare timber, Lugsy. That there widder-woman, she had some rare timber, di'n't she?"

And Lugsy, whose good manners had held the widow's attention for a mere fortnight, would beat his hand on his knee and cackle in genteel agreement.

Standard Four: 1928

One sunny spring day more than fifty odd years ago, a group of country children were marched from the class-room into the playground of the National school and posed there together for the photographer. It was, as I remember, the redoubtable Standard Four. They are there still, frozen in the picture on my wall, taken captives on that long ago day and kept safe and ever young, as if whatever could happen to them afterwards was of no importance. I knew them well, that odd, mixed bunch — and what lively, individual characters they were at around twelve years old despite the photo's frigid passivity.

Look at Shorty Lanham there, the thin, lanky boy in the back row with a collarless flannel shirt held at the neck by a very visible brass stud. Shirt collars were a problem for all, of course, but solved by careful mothers by using a washable celluloid kind or by the new, woollen guernseys which had a collar attached and were completed with a knitted tie striped horizontally. But these were fal-de-lals that had little place in the school lives of such as Shorty and his pals. On the few occasions that he had ever been constrained into wearing a collar it was obvious that it provided some special kind of torture for him. He wore an old loose jacket that was long enough to be taken for a coat, some cut-down corduroys and, in common with three or four of his cronies, sported a basic type of haircut that consisted of having the head shorn almost to the scalp except for a brush or fringe at the front. It was a local fashion that at least had the merit of limiting the area of exploration when the nurse came to search for nits.

Unfortunately, such examinations were generally fruitful. Untidy little Ruth Warne in the front row and lank-haired Annie King who looked ever pale and frightened, people said because of the blows that came from her drunken father, were sent home regularly to clean their hair. Not so Connie and Betty, sitting there like lovebirds in the very centre of the group, their ribbons slipping on to each other's shoulders. These two enjoyed one of those long, inviolable friendships that lasted through the entire period of their school days — Betty so clean and nervous, sitting even now as if she would run away and vanish were it not for staunch, old-fashioned Connie in her high boots and starch-white pinafore providing a clinging-place and a certainty in the noisy life of the school.

Joe, Hoss, Winkle and Kit sit together in a bunch, as you would expect. For once they are quiet, for once hatless. Joe's trousers, always so torn that they could never prevent his shirt-tails escaping, are mercifully out of sight but his rolled-up cloth cap looks out of his pocket. In those days being hatless was near enough to being naked.

These were my friends. We shared the thin benefits of elementary education in the twenties, made bleaker by the heavy hand of church dogma. Neither they nor I ever dreamed, or were encouraged to dream, of anything like equality in education or in any other part of our lives. We looked out of the windows of our thatched little school on to the swelling grounds and noble facade of a prominent grammar school but we never queried the reason for the

68

difference. Our place was God-given. Moreover, we couldn't have been happier with the arrangement.

When we left school we went to work as farm-boys, errand-boys, odd-job boys. The cleverest member of the class, Brassy Wilkinson, became a telegraph boy and the envy of everyone around with his official bicycle and uniform provided. The fact that such jobs were dead-end and monotonous had little significance for us in the twenties — in our situation we were meant for dead-end and monotonous jobs.

There is one child in that photograph that I remember with especial tenderness. Her name was Laura and she always seemed to me to be different from the others — more direct, more humorous, more daring. She was small and wore neat, dark clothes and black stockings and a round felt hat for school. Generally, she had two or three younger children hanging on to her coat and whenever I tried to walk home with her after school I was defeated by the sheer number of diminutive followers.

It was not until I was fourteen and had left school that I was able to see Laura regularly. On spring evenings I would cycle into the town and wait for her at the end of the street. After a time she would come out of the little house looking like a princess, rich with the promise of love and beauty. Sometimes we stood in the lights of the little fruit shop all the evening and her hair glistened and her voice was the loveliest sound in the world.

But that summer passed, as summers do. Laura went to work in a shop and I moved to another village some ten miles away. It was by chance that I met Laura one Sunday morning and we walked by the river and she promised that she would be loyal to me and not talk to other boys. She wrote to me almost next day — I kept the letter for a great many years until it fell into shreds — promising a rendezvous on her next free afternoon on Wednesday. It was something almost too perfect for the waiting to be borne. In good time on Wednesday I was at the meeting place and waiting. I waited and then searched wherever I thought she might be found — the streets, the river walk, the cinema, the road where she lived. I stopped children who might have seen her and neighbours who had the supreme privilege of living close by where she slept, but none knew of her whereabouts or were interested. I could not find her, not that day nor the next Wednesday nor ever again.

It is true, I think, to say that I never saw Laura again. But a long life-time produces many and usually unflattering changes. We who are old end up, not with triumphal organ-music but lost among the ash-cans, sunk in inconsequence and anti-climax. There is an old woman who lives within two miles of me now who says she is Laura. I know her to be Laura but it is of no significance. It is just an old woman with two cats and a snivel who does not even remember me. It is one of the enigmas of passing time that Laura was and is to me the girl in the photograph, happy and vital and promising to love me. What happens to us? Who is this old woman?

As with Laura, so with all the rest of Standard Four. I know what happened to most of them. In a separate compartment of my mind I know that they moved out of that frozen group in the photograph and grew up and became a different kind of people. Shorty Lanham must have taken to a collar eventually and Joe to trousers that concealed his shirt tails for they both took the army uniform, were captured at Singapore and did not return. Sergeant Hoss and Private Winkle also lost their lives

70

with honour at Arnhem. Frightened Annie King was 'put away' and several have died.

Yet to me this does not dispose of Standard Four. So far as I am concerned they are still the children in the picture. Whatever happened to them after, the twenties is where they belonged, where they were born and moulded, where they felt the sun that warm spring day and where they shouted their living gladness along the quiet lanes. How it was they came to grow old belongs to a different world altogether.

A Run From His Money

It would be difficult to pick a more idyllic spot for a visit on a fine summer's day than Letheringham Mill near Wickham Market, with its attractive setting and its hint of days gone by. Certainly it attracts a steady stream of visitors, not many of whom perhaps would give much credence to tales of clanking chains and ghosts thereabouts, but it is a fact that the Mill was the scene of a brutal double murder at one time in its history. Its association with a ghostly chase and a disappearing corpse is something that has to be left to individual beliefs. At least Mr. Gall, a one-time tailor of Wickham Market, swore that there was a ghost and he was in the best position to judge, being no more than a yard or so ahead of his phantom pursuer, as he reckoned, for the whole of his record-breaking run from the mill to his home.

But the story begins with the murder, which was real and dreadful enough. A Mr. Bullard ran the mill then with the help of his son and also, it seems, with the assistance for a time of a journeyman named Jonas Snell. Perhaps Snell was sacked, perhaps he had other real or imagined reasons for hating the father and son but whatever the motive, the day came when he could no longer restrain his thirst for vengeance. He killed them both at the mill, ran off but was soon caught and apprehended and six weeks later executed at Wickham Market.

In those days it was customary to exhibit the bodies of miscreants on gibbets for long periods of time. Local people had seen the figure hanging and swinging on

72

Poachards Green for so long that they no longer took much notice of it. Among them was Mr. Gall the tailor, a forthright and sceptical character well-known for his scoffing at such things as ghosts. Unlike more timid people, he had no qualms about taking that road and was even known to treat the gibbet with some levity, taking off his hat in mock salutation or even addressing a few words to the mute victim. In fact, he often found himself walking that particular route in the pursuit of his profession, which required him to go forth with patterns and tape measure to attend the gentry and wealthy farmers in their own homes.

On the day of his abject change of mind about ghosts, he had set out in the morning to walk the couple of miles to Letheringham Mill where he was due to do some work. In good humour and as self-assured as ever he came to the gibbet at Poachards Green and was reckoning how long the body had hung there in its chains. He paused and looked up at the figure and said aloud: "I see you're still up there in your exalted position. What about getting down from there today?" He chuckled and went on, forgetting about the incident since he was engrossed for most of the day in cutting and measuring at the mill. Darkness had fallen before his task was finished but he set off for home well satisfied with his day's work.

His sense of well-being lasted as far as Poachards Green but there the bleak open-ness of the green emphasised the wind and the darkness and he pulled his cloak closely about him as he walked past the gibbet. By habit he looked up but in the darkness could not see the body — nor could he hear the chains. He stopped, and with a strange fear suddenly seizing him, went up close to the gibbet. The body was gone — so were the chains. The sudden disappearance after his taunting words in the morning drove Mr. Gall to see a calculated design in the matter, a ghastly reproof for his scepticism. The gibbet with a body was something tolerated without much difficulty but a gibbet that suddenly lost its body and its chains left the space full of strange and horrible possibilities.

Mr. Gall began to walk quickly, his dignity and assurance dwindling with every step he took, anxious to get away from the area. As he hurried, he began to be aware of the sound of chains close behind him, scarcely noticeable at first but as he quickened his pace the sound increased. The faster he ran, the closer the chains seemed to follow. Along the dark roads he ran, afraid to pause for breath until he staggered at last into Wickham Market street, his strength exhausted and his dignity in shreds. When his wife received him, abjectly shaking with fear, into their home, he assured her that he was a changed man. No longer would he scoff at talk of ghosts or such things for he knew now only too well that they existed. So worn out and beaten was the poor tailor that he went straight to his bed and his wife came and helped him remove his clothes.

In a back pocket of his coat she found there was a handful of coins and a thimble or two and as she moved the coat and shook it she must have smiled a wifely smile as she recognised how nearly the sound was to the sound of chains.

The body had been removed by the authorities during the day while the tailor was busy at Letheringham Mill.

A Rise For Frank

The boys' father came into their bedroom soon after daylight, shook the rail of the iron bedstead nearest to the door and went out again. The shaking dislodged the only brass knob left on the posts and it rolled and rattled on the bare floor between the two beds.

Frank, the oldest of the brothers, and Arnie slept in the near bed and it was they who had been given the peremptory signal to arise. The two younger boys in the other bed could stay there for the time being. When they had grown big enough to lift a sack of potatoes, push a barrowload of manure or use a spade and fork on the land, their time would come to turn out and work on the smallholding with the others.

Frank, one eye open, caught a glimpse of his father disappearing out of the door, collarless and unshaven, to return to the kitchen to boil up the kettle over the sticks in the stove. Their mother would have arisen, too, but in the early years of the twenties the demands of stays and petticoats, pinned-up hair and buttoned boots were lengthy even for a woman who would spend the whole day in nothing but labour. However, when she appeared in the kitchen she would take over at once, pour out the smoke-flavoured tea and urge the two boys not to dawdle but to follow their father into the yard as quickly as possible.

It seemed to Frank that his father was always disappearing ahead of him and that they never really caught him up. By the time he had scalded his throat with the tea and gone out his father would be moving on again, poultry-house to pig-sty, pig-sty to stable, silently leaving him jobs to finish.

It was a race throughout the day to keep up, to try and show his father his own strength and growing importance. Even in the evening when the family sat about the kitchen table his father was still ahead, projecting his thoughts towards tomorrow and the next day or he would be hidden behind a newspaper, not just reading it but searching it for some guide-lines to his hard life.

Nevertheless, Frank had decided that he must confront his father very soon on the question of a rise. His wages were a theoretical ten shillings a week, half of which was handed to him when work ended at mid-day on Saturday and the rest added to the house-keeping allowance

Of the five shillings that Frank received, half-a-crown was religiously put aside for buying clothes and with the half-crown remaining he went to the pictures once a week, smoked four packets of five Woodbines and bought a quarter pound of expensive sweets — sixpence a quarter — buttered brazils were his favourite — at the shop where the pretty girl served.

Considering that Frank, at sixteen, was capable of doing most of a man's work it seemed little enough after two years of such a budget. Another shilling a week would make things look much more cheerful. One evening Frank took his courage in both hands and spoke to the top of his father's head as he saw it above the newspaper.

"I'd like a little more money, father," he said, trying not to mumble or to allow his voice to shake. He felt the quiet in the room, his mother not raising her eyes from

76

her darning but the younger boys tense and listening. His father searched a whole page through before he answered: "You would, eh?"

"Well, now I'm sixteen —"

"Sixteen, eh? Well, well, is that what you are?" He exhibited a naive surprise as he put the paper down and looked over the top of his glasses. Mother had bought the glasses for him from Woolworth's for sixpence and they magnified wonderfully but scarcely reached his size so that he could hook them on to only one ear at a time. Just the same, he looked formidable enough to keep everyone waiting with bated breath.

"You know what my owd mother would ha' said ter me at yar age?" he asked at last. "She'd ha' said you ain't got the cradle marks off yar backside yit."

He pushed his tea-cup away and went back to his paper. "Where's my other cup o' tea?" he complained. "That last one was jest like pond-water."

Frank's mother brought the tea-pot from the hob where it was warming. Frank would have spoken again but his mother nudged him to indicate that he must now drop the subject or continue at his peril.

"Y'see, tha's in his mind now," she told Frank next day. "He 'on't forgit — but don't yew ask him agin. He's got ter give ut of his own accord. He'll come round tew ut ef he think yo're wuth an extra shillin' or tew."

But Frank, and Arnie who was a year younger, were both at an impatient age. They mumbled and muttered as they worked and slept together and their mother watched them anxiously as she watched her husband. She was ever the cushioning influence, the mediator on whom no decisions rested yet all depended.

It was she who saw the signs of revolt turn into a plan of

escape to a less demanding kind of life. The army, she guessed, and if it was to be the army then it would have to be on a Friday for the recruiting office opened only on that day in the small town nearby. In the quiet of their bedroom she told her husband of her fears. "Tha's the army they've set their minds on," she said. "I reckon they'll run off one o' these days."

He did not answer. He lay in the bed and stared at the grey light of the window and she knew how inside he curled up with the hurt. He would not say aye or nay to any son old enough to make his own decisions but he felt some of the will and the warmth of life drain away in the wordless silence. Next day, their mother was sharp when she saw the boys.

"Yew shou'n't ought ter be thinkin' o' goin' an' leavin' yar father like that," she told them, her own grief taking second place. "He work his guts out ter keep this family tergither — haps yew'll remember that when yew git inter that owd army."

For all that, the two boys pursued their plan. On Friday morning they fed the stock as usual, then, when they should have gone into the orchard to mow, they crept back into the house, changed to their going-out clothes and set off on the long walk into town.

They felt uncomfortable and in a hurry to get it over. Arnie was worried. One of the pigs was sick, he said. Frank was shocked. "Din't yew tell father?" he asked.

"We'd never ha' got away. He'll find ut sune enough — yew know father. We got ter forgit about pigs now, Frank."

It was easier said than done. The sick pig followed them like the ghost of conscience itself to the very threshold of the recruiting office. Inside was the most resplendent army sergeant they had ever seen and they stared through the window, at once fascinated and wary. At the back of their minds was the inescapable thought that, majestic as he was, the sergeant would never understand their concern over an ailing pig.

"We'll atter go back," said Frank. "Case he don't find that pig. That might be somethin' that'll spread t' the others."

"Ef tha's eeriesyphilis that will," agreed Arnie.

When they got back to the holding their father was dosing the pig. He looked up as they climbed into the pen to help to hold the pig still. "I reckon tha's on'y a chill," he said. "That'll be up an' right as rain tomorrer."

The two boys leaned against the pig-sty rails and watched their father and the pig. It was good to be back and to breathe the old familiar smells. "We bin out," said Frank ashamedly, "we bin out inter the town. We was a-goin' ter join up —"

"We atter come back cause o' the pig," added Arnie.

Their father looked at them, wiping his hands. "Fine pair o' soldiers yew tew make," he observed, "still, ef you've finished yar turn o' duty with the forces I got plenty for yew ter dew round here".

"I know we shou'n't ha' gone off like that —" Frank said. For once, his father paused in his work as if some chord in his memory was stirred "I know how yew feel," he said quietly, "I bin young meself once. Yew ain't the first young boys ter feel they had ter try an' kick over the traces. Come ter think on't," — his bantering tone returned but the boys resented it no longer and smiled — "come ter think on't, a spell in the army might ha' done yew tew a bit o' good."

Later he came into the orchard and helped them cock

79

the hay. "I bin thinkin'," he told them, wiping the beads of sweat from his face, "yew boys ain't had a rise lately. I reckon yew both 'arn another couple o' bob a week now."

The Gleaners

Sarah came in from the gleaning when the mill hooter said noon. Her four children came too, subdued and dirty, avils still clinging to their hair and dust smudged into the sweat streaks on their faces.

In the cottage they made straight for the open pail of drinking water standing on the cool floor of the scullery. Sarah carried the heavy sack of shelled corn and broken ears into the pantry.

"Don't yew drink tew much o' that cowd water," she shouted. She threw off her old coat as she went into the kitchen and clicked open the fire-door of the range. It was long cold: the ash began to spill out on to the bricks as she lifted the fire bars.

"Git me some kindlin', Alfie," she called. "Alfie — yew git some sticks afore yew feed that ferret. Yer father'll be hoom sune an' no dinner riddy."

The mention of his father was enough. The oldest boy swung out of the back door and went down the narrow garden path to the woodshed where the chopping block and pile of faggots were the all too familiar accompaniments of his labours. From the corner of the shed he grabbed an untidy armful of sticks and dribbled them all the way along the path to the house, depositing what was left on the rug in front of the fire stove.

"Now yew git that ferret fed," Sarah told him. Urgently, she rebuilt and lit the fire, marking with black streaks the hands and wrists that were already dust-covered from the gleaning. "That 'on't ever heat the oven in time," she thought — but she could heat up the rabbit stew and make some dumplings and hope he would forget that he had the same thing yesterday.

The stove began to roar and suck at the flames: in no time the bars were red and the kitchen an inferno in which summer flies fussed and buzzed.

Sarah called to the children to wash themselves at the pump outdoors and took a bowl full of the ice-cold water and a square of yellow soap to the limited privacy of the kitchen sink for herself. She felt stiff from bending in the stubble and wretched with dirt and untidiness.

When she had finished, she patted her hair straight and took the water to spill on the garden. Then, as she stirred the stew over the flaring range, he was there, with heavy boots slow on the path outside then clumping over the scrubbed brick floor of the scullery. She glimpsed out of the corner of her eye the corduroys tied with binder twine below the knee and the old wide hat that would stay on his head until, as if disarming himself, he would show his wispy, tired head to his family as he sat down to the table.

Sarah fed him quickly, thinking how she would tackle him about the new clothes and about the Sunday School Treat. You never knew how Fred was going to take things — especially if he was in one of his awkward moods. She eyed him carefully, biding her time. As it happened, nothing seemed to try his temper today; he was quiet and more thoughtful than usual.

"I heard they was a-goin' to drum the river hare today," he said at last. "Tha's suffen I ain't heard of since I was a nipper. They reckon that 'ere lairy boy — Martha Watson's boy — they reckon he must ha' drownded his self in the river. They can't fare to find him anywhere else

— so this arternoon they're a-goin' to drum all along o' the river from the lock to Harley's Farm. Policemen'll beat the drum."

Sarah said shortly: "I reckon that's interferin' in things what ought to be left. Ef that poor daft boy is in the river there ain't no drum'll bring him back to life agin — that I dew know."

"Haps tha's a merciful relief in a way," Fred agreed. "That boy — he was a cruel crorse for poor owd Martha to bear all on her own."

"Well, tha's the will o' God," said Sarah primly. As soon as the meal was ended she whispered to Alfie and he went out. When he reappeared a few minutes later he was dressed uncomfortably in a tolerably new Norfolk jacket, with a hard celluloid collar and short corduroy trousers.

He stood on the tiny stage formed by the rag rug and backed by the hot stove and faced his father. Sarah was on her knees, fingering the strong material and as proud as if she had made the garments herself.

"Jest feel that clorth, father," she said. "That'd dew for Alfie for nigh on the rest o' his school days."

Fred look suspiciously at the boy, the new clothes and his wife. "Hev somebody give yew them cl'oes?" he asked.

"They ain't bin give — I'm a-buyin 'em for five shillin's." Sarah hesitated but realised she would have to tell the full story. "They belonged to Martha's boy. She brought 'em up to the gleanin' field this mornin'. She give me the fust chance to buy 'em."

Fred said wonderingly: "Martha's boy? That poor boy they're a-searchin' for? Why, they don't even know ef he's a goner yit."

83

Sarah looked at him, half ashamed but determined. "That ain't no use pretendin', Martha say. Young Tom, he was allust sorft enough to walk inter the river an' git drownded. They 'on't find him alive now, Martha say. That's the will o' God, she say."

"Will o' God! That fare to me yew women-folk yew push the will o' God the way yew want it to go sometimes."

"Tha's blasphemous, father. Yew know that ain't no good pretendin' that 'ere owd drum 'll bring the boy back." Sarah turned back to the clothes displayed on the wilting Alfie. "'Sides, they'll come in jest right for the Treat."

In the afternoon when Fred had returned to work, Sarah went back to the field to continue gleaning. Martha was there picking up on the side of the field from which she could see a stretch of the river and Sarah came and worked beside her.

"Did he say yes to them clo'es?" asked Martha.

"Well, he di'n't say no — an' tha's as much as I'm likely to git. Anyway, I ha' brought the five shillin's from the savin's." Sarah held out her hand with the two half-crowns but Martha said: "Dew yew howd that till they ha' gone up the river wi' the drum. That don't seem right till they ha' done that."

At three o'clock there came the first muffled sound of the drum from far off down the river and the two women stood up long enough to identify the sound. During the next hour, as they went on gleaning, the sound became a regular, strong beat that rolled sonorously over the fields and went on and on as if it were a solemn comment on all mortality.

Martha stood and pointed. Slowly along the middle of

84

the river came the rowing boat. The village constable was seated in the stern, regularly striking the drum that rested on his knees.

"What dew that dew, then," whispered Sarah, half scared herself at the solemn ritual. "Dew that bring dead bodies to the top?"

"Some say that dew," said Martha sadly. "Others — they say tha's done to find the body, 'cos when tha's near, the sound o' the drum change."

They stood together and waited, their hands still clutching ears of corn. They heard and felt the drum go on loud and solemn as if it were their own heart-beats, all the way up to the lock. Towards the lock the sound grew faint but it did not change. Then it stopped suddenly and the river and the fields were very quiet.

Martha stood for a little, then bent her back again for the gleaning. "They've gone," she said. "I may as well hev that five shillin's now."

Aginst The Burrowcrats

Not many people have been referred to in their own lifetime as a village Hampden or as a rural Churchill. To be truthful, it did not quite happen to Sidney Buttle, since East Anglians are not given to that kind of eulogy, but it came very close when the landlord of the Plough called him "old partner" and gave him free drinks on the house. Others agreed that Sidney certainly had his head screwed on properly and more than one now called him "Mister."

The period of Sidney's ascendancy was that in which the village found itself fighting for survival. For too long the local people had mellowed with the old houses, unconcerned that new houses were never built there; that the farms no longer supported more than a handful of men or that the school that had once hugged over a hundred children to its bosom was now deserted and nearly derelict.

There had been but a slight feeling of apprehension when the news came that the new road would by-pass the village and take away the only bus. But when the row of old cottages in the street became condemned, the villagers came face to face with the fact that very soon there would be no village left.

In response to a growing demand to know what the parish council was going to do about it, an extraordinary meeting was called. It took place on a mild October evening only five years ago and was held in the Hut, which was a timber-built victory symbol of the Great

War, improved by the additions of toilets and hessian curtains in the flush of another victory in 1945.

This historic meeting promised at first to be the usual babel of inanities of parish meetings. There were older folk tirelessly recalling the happier days of yore when farms had men to work instead of machines: an argument began as to whether there were 15 or 25 men employed on Summerfield Farm in 1930 and this led somehow to the mention of badgers. Tom Richards had strong thoughts on the subject: "Them creatures hev jest as much right to live as anybody else. I don't recollect that a-sayin' in the Bible as how the food o' the world was jest for human beans."

Charlie Scopes stood up and said he agreed. He always gave his hens free range and would never put them in cages whatever anyone said. Mrs. Grimston said that now the nights were drawing in they had to think of Christmas and the New Year.

With the patience of past experience, the chairman waited till all views had been aired then indicated that he had before him the draft of a strong letter which, with their permission, he intended to send to the various councils and authorities in any way concerned.

The village must remain viable, said the chairman, rather pleased at having thought of this word. They needed houses and a community centre and more buses and even a small factory would help to make things more — er — viable.

Someone pointed out that they had already sent such a letter and nothing had happened. They had not even had a reply. But, everyone agreed, it was the only thing they could do — to keep at the throats of the higher authorities like mastiffs.

"No," said a voice at the back of the hall. It was Sidney, grasping the nettle danger in both clammy hands. "No."

"No?" said the chairman. People looked round in annoyance at the least significant person present. "Sit down," they shouted.

"No," repeated Sidney, red-faced but confident that this was the most important moment of his life. "Don't yew send that there letter. That'll only put us at the mercy o' the burrowcrats an' tha's jest what they want. I reckon this is our big opportunity. Yew say this village ha'nt changed in a hundred years — well, tha's fantastic. There's a place in Australia —"

There was a considerable demand from the long-suffering villagers in the hall for Sidney to shut up. "In Australia —" he tried again.

"Australia don't come under our jurisdiction," the chairman told Sidney sternly.

"In Australia," persisted Sidney, knowing it was now or never, "thousands of people travel from all over jest to see one little owd village. Tha's a place no different from this — a village jest as that was tew hundred year ago. An' people come from all over to see it."

Suffolk people being what they are it was impossible to tell immediately whether Sidney's message had been well received or not — or even if it had been understood. But they were quiet and thoughtful as they went home and during the next week Sidney was called on to put his idea into more detail before a parish committee. In November another extraordinary meeting was held at which Sidney took the honoured place between the chairman and the schoolmaster.

After the preliminary hubbub during which Tom Richards held up a Bible and demanded to know where it said that human beans had the right to kill badgers and Mrs. Grimston remarked that the nights were drawing in, Sidney was called on with some deference to put his plan to the assembly.

"If we all work together," Sidney told them, "we can make this place the envy o' the whool country — an' bring in an income tew. Only we ha' got to go back stid o' forrard an' make the village jest like that was tew hundred year ago. That ain't all that difficult. Mr. Rogers, our schoolmaster, he know all the history an' he say the whool place is based on the eighteenth century."

Sidney went on to elaborate his scheme. If everybody helped they could throw open the village as an eighteenth century tourists' Mecca on each Saturday during the coming summer.

In the meantime there was a lot of work for everyone, partly in hiding up the evidences of the present day. The smithy at the end of the street would be opened up and Jacob Bloss could still make a good show of skill there. A couple of horses would be tethered nearby for atmosphere. The old bakery could be used in a rota by the women in turning out bread and the food of that time.

Then there was the tithe barn on Summerfield Farm which could be used as a demonstration museum of past agricultural methods. Stocks could be made to stand on the green where stocks had stood long ago and a maypole could be put there too.

"A maypole, — tha's Elizabethan," shouted some know-all.

"It would be quite in order," the schoolmaster decided, "to show objects belonging to periods before the eighteenth century but not after." He went on to say that he thought the great attraction would be the row of pretty houses where Mrs. Grimston lived, for they were without doubt old spinning and weaving cottages. They needed one or two spinning wheels, replicas would do, and the good ladies could sit outside on open days spinning or carding or combing the wool.

"I reckon tha's a daft idea," shouted Fred Baynes, who objected on principle because Sidney was a neighbour of his.

For a few weeks Sidney strode like a king through the village street. Then suddenly, for the third and last time, another extraordinary meeting was called. At this meeting Sidney was no longer on the stage, nor was the schoolmaster. The chairman read out a letter he had received from the planning authority.

"After long discussion," the letter said, "we have agreed to your repeated requests for modernisation of the village. Plans are already in hand to build 24 houses, a central car park and community centre. It is possible that the new road, too, will come through the village."

A Childhood Memory

That autumn afternoon the teacher lit the gas lamps early, standing on the desks to reach the brackets. One after another the round globes burst into light with a gentle plop and the classroom was filled with the simmering glow.

"You can put your pens away and fold your arms," he said. He was a surprising man — we never knew quite how to take him. The scratching of nibs on exercise books eased up and we sat up straight, hollowing our backs for balance on the flat, backless forms. There were five of us sitting on my form. Ethel Forman sat next to me on one side and Tich Cole on the other. I liked Tich but I was not at all sure about Ethel Forman. She was rough — there were warts on her fingers and holes in the toes of her boots. I only looked at her when she wasn't looking at me.

The teacher was standing in front of the fire as he always did. He was a youngish man with a serious face and weak-looking eyes.

"There will be no more writing today," he said. "Instead, we shall do some drawing. And the girls can practise their tableaux for Empire Day."

Two boys dropped their arms from the folded position in an ecstasy of surprise and to restore order he made them stand with their hands on their heads. The rest of us kept very quiet as the teacher handed out pieces of white paper, pencils and rubbers. He went to a cupboard, brought out a vase and stood it on a pile of books.

"You can begin," he said.

The two boys who had been standing with their hands on their heads were summoned to the teacher's desk. He looked at them as if he were considering a suitable punishment then let them off with no more than saying the Apostles' Creed and the Catechism from memory. What with this and the drawing lesson, you could tell it was a special day. There was no cane, no biting words, no bad temper. We all knew why. He was going off to the war the very next day and perhaps would never come to teach us again.

We set about sketching the vase. The clean, white paper took the first tentative lines, then the new lines that corrected the old ones, then yet more wavering lines and more rubbing and scrubbing until the paper dimmed and rucked and showed nothing at all except a conglomeration of finger marks. As the flecks of rubber built up in drifts round our elbows the teacher came round to look but no one got the expected rap on the knuckles. He just looked at the drawings and said nothing.

Ethel Forman and three or four other girls had gone out to prepare for the tableaux and now they came back draped in flags and pieces of muslin to represent Empire countries.

"I am India," said Ethel and pulled the bit of muslin across her face to show that it was an eastern veil. It got into her mouth and muffled the piece she had to say about India being a jewel in our crown. But I thought she looked very nice. Perhaps it was because she had taken off her high buttoned boots and her hair was light and combed. She looked soft and different in the wisps of muslin and I decided that I liked her after all.

Then it became very quiet in the classroom as the clock neared the time of dismissal. The tableau had settled down to being merely a tableau and we could scrub no longer at our dingy sketches. As the gas jets hummed the teacher came round quietly and collected the papers while the monitors counted the pencils and rubbers. Then we stood in the hazy warmth and put our hands together and said: "Lighten our darkness we beseech thee O Lord and by thy great mercy defend us from all the perils and dangers of this night." We ended in a whisper because the teacher had stopped leading us half way through. He was looking down at the floor as if he had forgotten the words. Afterwards he raised his head, nodded to the monitor on the front form and told us to follow out quietly and go home. We looked at him as we filed past but there was nothing for us to say and anyway he was busy collecting his books together and seemed not to notice us.

Then we were out and free! Conkers had fallen from the great horse-chestnuts during the day and there was a rush to pick them up. Some of us raced for the clump of beeches a short distance along the road. There was already a mass of children, boys and girls together, grubbing around for the nuts. Ethel was there already. When I came up she held her closed fists towards me. "I got these for you," she said. Her hands were full of beech nuts and the rough, triangular husks clung to her wet palms as she emptied them into mine.

We stood together against the school wall, eating the beech nuts. Most of the other children had gone but half a dozen boys suddenly came running past, laden with conkers.

"Bombardment!" one of them shouted and they

repeated the word excitedly one after another. It was a word that had sifted back from the trenches and was a favourite with boys at that time. "Bombardment! We'll bombard the teacher when he goes past." They took up hiding places behind a hedge and Ethel and I joined them there. We would bombard the teacher as he went home — there was nothing he could do about it now.

As we waited, the road became very still and the dusk began to settle in the trees. The teacher came out of the school gate and began to walk towards us, carrying his heavy case of books. "Bombardment!" the boys whispered, with their hands full of conker ammunition but we only looked at the teacher as he went past. He was struggling with the case and he looked small and wispy and alone. He would never kill any Germans, I thought. He would be useless out there in the front lines: the Huns would chop him into little pieces.

The conkers fell from our hands and we came out from behind the hedge and watched him until he was almost out of sight. Then Ethel suddenly shouted "Goodbye, sir," and ran a little way down the road as if to try and make him hear. Then all the boys yelled "Goodbye, sir," but it was too late. He did not turn round and we never saw him again.

Potatoes For A Bride

"Ef yew call to mind," old George Garrott said ponderously as the last of a small convoy of vehicles bound for the wilder reaches of the Broads sped past the bench at the roadside. "Ef yew call to mind, I was jest a-goin' to tell yew suffen about my taters."

Freddie-Boy coughed out the dust and prompted the older man respectfully. "Fat hin. Tha's what yew was a-sayin" — about fat hin."

"Ah, tha's right," agreed George, with the magnanimity of one long accustomed to victory in the field of champion vegetables, "I was sayin' about fat hin. Yew nearly allust git that owd weed a-growin' along o' taters. Tha's that grut seedy-lookin' thing — that'll grow a yard high dew that git half a chance."

Freddie-Boy swallowed his pride and a little more dust as he listened patiently. The old man was foxing again. Anyone knew what fat hen was and he didn't want a lecture about that. But such was George's standing in the potato show world you had to allow him the privilege of mentioning academic matters in any discussion about the prime vegetable. The irritating thing was that he kept amateurs like Freddie-Boy in the dark about the real secrets of his success.

It irked Freddie-Boy that, as a mere novice with a record of Highly Commendeds, he could see no way of toppling George from his pedestal of achievement. First prize three years running at the local flower show and everything looking as if it would be the same result this

95

year — it was a maddening situation. He had been toadying around the complacent George today to the extent of sharing the bench at the dusty roadside in the hope that the old man might let slip something about his methods. It was all to no avail but it increased Freddie-Boy's determination to get the better of George. No matter that his achievements so far had been mediocre, ambition coloured his dreams with promised glory.

In fact, the matter had lately reached some urgency for he was now betrothed to the attractive Mary Hollins, whose father had once claimed the admiration of the show world by the perfection of his red beet. It was not surprising that in the course of Freddie-Boy's courtship, the question of potatoes often rose between them. It was not good enough for Mary, he decided, that he should go to the altar still in the Highly Commended class. Only the highest accolade would be adequate.

In this, as it happened, he quite misunderstood Mary's view of the matter. Like other ambitious gardeners, he absorbed others into his enthusiasms and failed to realise that Mary not only had no dreams of potato prizes but that, if anything in a vegetable show inspired her at all, it was the music of the words Highly Commended. Perhaps if Freddie-Boy had been less wrapped up in his horticultural ambitions and more attentive to Mary's moods, he would have noticed a distinct falling-off in warmth whenever the subject of prize vegetables came up. Instead, he continued on his blinkered way, convinced that George Garrott could provide the key both to potato triumphs and married happiness. So he used guile to corner the old man and blatant flattery coupled to sly questions in order to get him to reveal the vital secrets.

In fact, he gained nothing at all from his efforts, learning only the one thing — apart from the fact that George was becoming intolerably pompous about his successes — that George depended upon a certain strain of potato. But what that strain was, the champion refused to tell.

During the months that followed, Freddie-Boy's courtship of Mary was interwoven with schemes to beat the champion. One day he had the brilliant idea of sending a small boy to buy some potatoes at George's door, hoping that he might be selling off some of his specials as cooking potatoes but the plan misfired. George not only had no potatoes for sale but managed to wheedle from the boy the identity of the person who had sent him. Freddie-Boy's gloom deepened even more now when the two men met, for the swords were out of their scabbards and George used his advantage to tease the younger man with a deluge of advice while keeping his real secrets to himself.

However, there suddenly appeared as if from nowhere — actually from a commercial traveller who had left it on the bar of the village pub as a novelty — a single potato of such shapely proportions and delicate skin that proclaimed it to be of champion progeny. The super-potato was handed about in the bar for a day or two until some desperate negotiations brought it into Freddie-Boy's possession. It was a break-through at last. There was still time, he exulted, to plant and nurture this phenomenon so as to produce off-spring that would be certain to beat all comers.

Unfortunately, what should have been unalloyed joy for Freddie-Boy was upset at about that time by a quarrel with Mary. Her patience had given way at last and in the course of a rather heated exchange of words over future priorities in the marital home she had made it clear that if their relationship was to be as potato-ridden as it had been in the past, there would be no marital home because there would be no wedding. He could choose which prize he wanted — a first in potatoes or herself.

It was a considerable blow to Freddie-Boy. He thought the matter over very carefully while the super-potatoes flourished in his garden and produced even bigger and better tubers than the original, bigger and better than he had dreamed possible. Mary waited.

When the day of the Show came at last Freddie-Boy selected and cleaned six of the finest specimens and carried them to the produce tent. George was there already, his near-perfect potatoes resting in a dish in front of him, preening himself in anticipation of the glory that was bound to come and already scoffing at the offerings of other exhibitors. He stopped in mid-sentence when he saw the potato that Freddie-Boy produced and held tauntingly under his nose. Then another and another.

George stared in a daze. There had never been potatoes like this before. Freddie-Boy staged them in a dish and told George grandly: "Yew might git a second prize, haps, considerin' you ha' done the best yew can wiv a poor crop." He stood back to admire his exhibit and there were gasps from the few onlookers.

"That is to say," he went on, "ef I decide to show 'em." To George's astonishment he began to take the potatoes out of the dish and return them to his pocket. "As that happen, I don't choose to show 'em this toime — tha's tew easy in a little owd village like this. But o' course I may decide tew some other toime. Dew yew keep that in yar moind."

He began to walk out of the tent taking the super-potatoes with him. "Don't yew be afraid," he told the awestruck George, "to come an' ask me for advice ef yew ever want to know anything about growin' taters."

Then, as if as an afterthought, he turned back and filled the dish from another pocket of his best ordinary potatoes. Later the same day he gladdened Mary's heart with a beautiful certificate that said 'Highly Commended".

Village Artist

If one were to start at the very beginning, it would be necessary to go back to a day now beyond living memory — though described to me once by my Uncle Henry — the day when the village school opened and compulsory education began.

That was the day when children went to school for the first time by law. They came from all parts of the village, unhappily trudging out of the quiet morning to stand stiffly in the playground like cattle in a pound — frozen with apprehension.

Among these early pupils, although they did not yet know of each other's existence, were two boys and a girl who were to have a close association for the rest of their lives. One — the only one I came to know myself, when he was in his middle years — was my Uncle Henry, then eight years old; the girl was Lucy someone-or-other from one of the large village families. The third member of this trio was Alec Moss, the dealer's only son, a boy quick to grasp whatever was to his advantage, a regular sharper of a lad.

No two boys could have been more opposite in character, for Henry was slow, meditative and often in trouble with the teacher for dreaming and not paying attention to the lessons. Yet the two became fast friends, supported and complemented each other and each saw a quality in the other that he himself lacked and admired.

School life for all three was little better than they had

feared. Lucy, however, devoted herself to the demands of this strange new life and soon became a favourite, while Alec developed a surface facility which not only sufficed to keep him out of trouble but actually won him prizes for such achievements as reciting a whole chapter of the Bible or saying the Lord's Prayer backwards.

But even for these two, their success did little to mitigate the harsh monotony of learning by rote, while Henry, of slower intellect, found the whole thing intolerable. His only relief, when he could not comprehend or could not face the thought of all the future hours and days of repressive discipline, was to take out a pencil stub and draw something.

It was a kind of doodling at first — an activity that provided an escape for his imagination — and always done at considerable risk of getting the cane. However, Henry had graduated from scraps of paper to drawing in a penny exercise book before he was caught in flagrant disregard of the arithmetic lesson. By this time his doodling had begun to have some purpose and he was trying to sketch some of the things around him.

He was fascinated, not by what he could draw so much as what he could not — the gulf that haunts those who seek perfection in any undertaking. By infinite practice he had learned some of the mysteries of the craft and on this particular day was absorbed in sketching the bent figure of the boy in front of him.

The cane came down on his knuckles with the shock of surprise as well as of pain. The pencil and note-book were scattered as Henry was yanked to his feet and dragged to the front of the class. There the teacher sarcastically demonstrated Henry's ignorance of arithmetic before giving him six strokes across the hand.

It was the beginning of an oppressive and often cruel persecution by the teacher, himself bound by the system that considered that any deviation from the set work in the three R's was wicked and had to be stamped out.

Perhaps another boy than Henry would have given up the nonsense of sketching after that but Henry could not do so. As caning became more frequent so did his obstinate obsession with pencil and paper and the teacher found that his avowed intention to 'beat it out of him' caused only a sullen apathy. Henry came to the end of his career at school at the age of thirteen with little more to show than piles of scrap paper covered with drawings and hands that were sore from being caned.

For a time the trio became separated as they set out on their working lives, each of them following a predictable role. Alec went to work in the town as a shop boy and Lucy entered domestic service. As inescapably, Henry found a job on a local farm in the work he wanted to do. From time to time Alec or Henry would meet Lucy on her evening off and walk the footpath down to the river. Alec had become a personable and sophisticated young man with a promising future — but it was the modest, rough-handed Henry whom Lucy eventually accepted as her lover.

It was during their courtship that Henry did the bulk of the sketches that Lucy hoarded in her room, as well as the water-colours that he had learned to paint. In those years Henry saw everything with an artist's eye and despite the growing demands of manual work, was never happier than when painting with Lucy beside him.

When they were both twenty-one, Lucy and Henry were married and to secure a man's wages and the cottage they needed he took a job on a different farm. A few days after he began to work there he was eating his mid-day snack under a hedge and indulging in his habit of sketching while he ate, when the farmer appeared. The new boss seemed affable enough and exchanged a few remarks about the weather and the state of the soil before he caught sight of the sketch in Henry's lap.

Suddenly his face became sour, his manner hostile. It was obvious that he considered that such a pastime did not suit a really dedicated farm-worker and that its alien values would spoil a man for work with the plough. Henry sat thinking and looking at the sketch after the farmer had gone. With his new wife and a baby coming and his own proficiency still to be proved, he could not afford to annoy his new employer in the hard times that everyone was having. Even more important, the cottage went with the job and he must try to keep that at any price.

Besides, as a true son of the soil he understood the farmer's attitude. For the first time in years all the guilt and shame that he had felt at school came flooding back. He did not want to be thought odd; to be singled out from his fellow-workers because of what they would con-sider to be a pretentious pastime. When he got home that evening Henry picked up all the pictures he could find — piles of sketches, the water-colours that Lucy loved, the few finished oil-paintings — and heaped them on the table. As it happened Alec had come to visit them and he and Lucy watched Henry's set face as he seemed about to throw the whole pile on the fire.

"No, that ain't right," Lucy restrained him, almost in tears. "That can't be right, Henry, throwin' away your talent. That's part o' your life, Henry, an' part o' mine. Leave 'em be. You'll feel different tomorrow."

Henry was assailed for a moment by a pain as poignant as if he were parting from a child. He said bitterly: "That ain't done nothin' but bring me trouble ever since I started school. Tha's suffen I got ter forgit. No one ain't goin' ter say I don't earn my wages. Ef yew want to keep them pictures, yew keep 'em, only don't ever let me see 'em agin."

Lucy sorted out all the pictures that she treasured and Alec took the rest. "The only one I want," said Henry, 'is that there big one. That'll dew ter stop the draught in the chicken hut winder."

In the years that followed, Henry was never seen again to put pencil or brush to paper. How difficult it was for him no one discovered but as his family grew he threw himself more and more into the demands of the farm and his garden. He became immersed in the crops and in the nature around, apparently forgetting the colour and vitality that once held him and seeing only as a countryman the slow miracle of growth.

Lucy, however, never forgot. She watched Henry become set and heavy-bodied, his hands too crabbed with labour ever to wield a pencil again. Sometimes she took out the pictures and looked at them, but while he was content she would never allude to that side of their lives again. In fact, it was Alec who nearly blew it all up again in their faces.

It was typical of Alec that he had had to discover the monetary worth of Henry's work. He had taken the pictures around securing a place in an exhibition here, a corner of a gallery there, until the peculiar, undisciplined quality of the work was known and wanted.

One day he came back to the cottage with a letter in his pocket from a dealer offering a good price for all pictures showing Henry's signature that he could find. It was a tremendous opportunity for all three of them and a vindication of Henry's long and painful apprenticeship.

But, sitting with Henry and Lucy in the evening and watching their slow cottage ways, he knew that Henry could never paint again and it would only open old wounds to mention it. He subtracted his commission from the amounts already paid to him for the pictures and wrote a cheque for the balance, giving it to the couple on the pretext that he had come into some money unexpectedly.

Lucy looked at Alec and guessed the truth but said nothing. Henry was contentedly lighting his pipe by the fire. "That beat me," he said, "how yew clever people git hold o' money — I never could! But 'ere, I never had no brains as yew well know."

Second Time Round

"Yew come on hoom, Charlie," old Mrs. Mayling used to call from her door. "Charlie, time yew come hoom." But Charlie never came so far as we could tell — in fact no one even seemed to know who he was.

As time went by we scarcely noticed it but sometimes on a still, summer evening the old lady would come out to her step and call vaguely as if she too had half forgotten who Charlie was. Anyway, she lived out of the village proper and almost out of knowledge in an ancient farmhouse hidden beyond the trees. She lived quite alone and seldom had a visitor though there was a man who rented a caravan in the grounds and did all sorts of chores around the house.

We could see him sometimes going to shop in an old rattletrap of a cart or mowing the long grass in front of the house. But for one reason or another we had little sight or sound of either of them until that summer of 1925. The only regular visitor to pass our house on the way to Mayling's was the doctor and, since our curiosity as to the identity of Charlie had long ago worn thin, there was little enough to provide us with any interest in that trio.

Yet they were odd enough, by all accounts. There was Mrs. Mayling with her eccentricities and failing wits, the grim, hired man who limped silently around the place and the doctor, who was himself a self-confessed anachronism. In the twenties we liked to believe that we were moving along the road of progress pretty fast, as indeed we were, but, right or wrong, the doctor would have none of it. He clung to the Victorian habits and beliefs we were rapidly leaving behind; a crusty old bachelor living alone in a great Georgian house that was dedicated to grandfather clocks, piles of books and dust.

Nothing would hurry the doctor nor would he allow anything to disturb his dignity. He drove out to his scattered patients in one of the earliest types of car at something like ten miles an hour, sitting high up above the polished brass, straight-backed and impregnable to modernity. Beside him in a long, white coat sat his attendant, a figure perhaps even more immobile and dignified than his master. He was never allowed to drive, only to accompany the doctor, occasionally opening a door for him to descend. Then he would get back to his seat as stiff and unmoving as if made of stone. He and the doctor and their ancient car were already behind the times, which was ushering in the nimble Morris Cowleys and Morris Oxfords as well as the Fords. Country patients who used to wait for the doctor to come used to say that the only good thing about his antiquated mode of travel was that you could hear him coming from a mile or more away.

We could hardly avoid knowing, therefore, that the doctor was a frequent visitor to Mrs. Mayling's. For a couple of years he attended her with what seemed increasing regularity and if time meant anything to him and to the stolid attendant who waited outside they would have to concede that the visits were also becoming longer.

For ourselves, living at the next farm along the road and the Mayling's only close neighbours, it was something of no particular concern to us — until one day when something of the mystery was brought into the open.

It was a bright, mid-morning hour when it happened. Two or three of us were in or near the farmyard at the time. Martin was standing by the water trough switching his manure-caked boots with a stick and watching the cows pass indolently out to the meadows. Ted was doing a spell with the chaff-cutter in the barn with Tiny to help turn the wheel and the foreman's wife was just coming down the ladder from the straw stack in her daily search for hens' nests and eggs.

At that moment, Mrs. Mayling appeared at the road-side gate and hesitantly walked along the short drive into the farmyard. We had never seen her close to before. She was not old at all but wispy and neglected looking. She came into the yard and peered around and we could hear her saying "Charlie?" half to herself as she wandered around looking into the sheds and among the implements and even mounted the ladder that the foreman's wife had just left.

Not knowing what to do in such a situation, we just stared like the country bumpkins we were until the familiar chugging noise brought the doctor, apparently in search of her. Immediately behind him came another figure, pedalling his bike as well as he was able to keep up with the doctor — that of the dour character who limped about the Mayling's place. He leaned his bicycle against the post and limped anxiously forward, overtaking the doctor shuffling along at a snail's-pace in the drive and hurrying into the yard. He, too, was no old man when you came to look at him but he seemed tired and worn.

Mrs. Mayling was still searching around, taking no notice of anyone. The doctor and the limping man had a few hurried words and the limping man walked up to the woman and deliberately placed himself in front of her.

For a few moments she looked hard at him as he stood still, one hand outstretched, then seemed to recall who he was.

"I was just looking to see if Charlie was about," she said almost apologetically. "He ain't come hoom yet." The limping man said nothing until she seemed about to move past him, then he took her arm gently and said: "I reckon if yew come along hoom an' make a cup o' tea he'll be along soon."

He led Mrs. Mayling away down the drive. As he passed the doctor he made a gesture of despair or resignation but did not stop. That was the only time, save one, that we saw Mrs. Mayling and the work of the farm soon went on as usual. The doctor stayed behind for a few minutes but was not one for communicating anything to non-professional people and we got nothing from him save an apology for the incident. However, he was not unwilling to stay and admire the ducks and geese and to have a friendly word about the growing crops, during which time I managed to have a conversation with his attendant at the gate, an individual more open and informative in speech than his appearance suggested.

Apparently Mrs. Mayling and her husband had been farming in another part of the county until there was an unfortunate accident with a tractor on which both happened to be riding at the time. Her husband had escaped with an injured leg and she with severe shock which apparently had caused some loss of memory. That was all there was to the background, really. The tragedy lay in the effect of the accident upon Mrs. Mayling's temperament and her memory. It seemed that, unable to recognise her husband after the accident, she had actually driven him from the house although some fragment of memory caused her sometimes to call or to seek out 'Charlie'. The doctor's part was only as a keen disciple of the new science of psycho-analysis, by which he hoped to bring the couple together again.

As the doctor's attendant and I were talking, the limping man came back along the lane to pick up his bike. I did not need to be told that this was indeed Charlie, the husband whom Mrs. Mayling searched for but did not recognise. I felt sorry for him, living without much hope of reconciliation on the mere fringe of his wife's existence.

Apparently at the unrehearsed confrontation at our farm that morning there had been a wild hope by both doctor and Charlie Mayling that the familiar farmyard surroundings might produce a dramatic recall of memory but nothing so fortunate had occurred. Obviously Mrs. Mayling still believed the limping man to be the friendly and helpful odd-job man and nothing more. There was nothing else for him but to resume the role and go back to his occupancy of the caravan.

Unused to such bizarre situations in our rather staid village, we soon put the matter out of our minds and the only thing to remind us of the farmyard incident was the passing of the doctor's car, as slowly but as regularly as ever, to the Mayling's. In our mistrust of the unusual it was a relief that we never had the Maylings on the farm again. Nevertheless, the affair did have a happy ending after all.

Whether the doctor's dabbling in psychology had any part in it or not is difficult to know but it seemed that Mrs. Mayling became less distraught and forgot to call for 'Charlie' any more. Instead, she fell in love with the man who had been her support and comfort all through the difficult years — her odd-job man. For the second time, with patience and understanding, he set out to woo and wed her again.

They were re-married in September, shortly before they left the village for good. For her it was a new romance and a new life; for him a happy resumption of the old.

Them Owd Owls

"That snew that winter," remembered Charlie, who preferred strong verbs and sometimes stronger adjectives, "that snew that 'ere hard yew cou'n't see no hedges nor yit anythin' else. One night that was a-blowin' an' a-drivin' an' that clumb up the walls o' these housen till we cou'n't see out o' the winders. We had a master-job gittin' the back door open next mornin'."

"When we did git out we cou'n't tell where the pathway was or the gate or nothin'. That was all snowed over. Poor owd uncle Arthur, he say dew yew come this hare way, he say, dew yew foller along arter me. He ha'n't hardly spook afore down he went."

"Coo, that made me laugh. I say, cor-blast I say, where ha' yew got tew, Arthur? Well, he was a-hollerin'. Yew cou'n't see nothin' on'm 'cept his hid. He say that's that bloomin' ditch, he say, yew lot must ha' moved it dew I wou'n't ha' fell in. Poor owd Arthur, he knew where the ditch was arter that. Funny thing, we still call that Arthur's ditch."

Charlie would tell you about that long winter and the odd things that happened in the snow while he sat on the bench in the sun in the garden of his cottage during the warm summer afterwards.

Perhaps the depth of the snow increased in his memory as time went by, as did the stature of many of his other tales. But he would always conclude by saying: "O' course, I wor'n't much more'n a nipper, them days," as if to indicate that any deviation from the truth must be put down to childish imagination and should not be held against him. In fact, no one did. You could not feel that Charlie's slight inflations were anything more than part of his natural expansiveness. Compared with his one-time neighbour, Bossy Paterson, he was a paragon of modesty.

Unfortunately, of course, the boastful type of character is not always of urban origin: rare though he may be, many a village has known or heard of such a one, standing out noisily among his modest neighbours. Bossy was a notable example and so was Miller Barnes from the next village.

According to Charlie, it was a kind of justice that Miller Barnes was eventually killed by his own mill sails, for with all the knowledge that he affected to have he should at least have known how to avoid such a fate. Bossy Paterson suffered no such sudden end, though it may have been wished for him on several occasions.

Bossy figured in one of Charlie's favourite stories about that long winter of snow. Apparently Charlie had long hankered to take Bossy down a peg or two but this was no easy thing to achieve. Paterson was the complete boss's man and the unofficial watch-dog for the squire as well as being a general busy-body with prior knowledge of every happening in the village.

However, Charlie bided his time, believing that the moment would soon come when Bossy's self-importance would prove his undoing. It was during the period of snow that the opportunity came.

Probably the most notable feature of this otherwise humble village was the grand entrance to the Hall. It was splendid enough for a much larger mansion and consisted of immense wrought-iron gates between tall brick pillars. Surmounting the pillars were two stone birds of prey. To the squire and his friends they were undoubtedly eagles but since such exotic birds could hardly be given credence by the villagers they were generally referred to as "them owls".

The squire would have preferred to have stone lions couchant but this thunder had been taken from him by the nearby stately home whose prior right to the lions couchant was clear. Anyway, the squire was content with eagles. They added considerable character to the place, he thought, and was more than a little put out when he heard that children regularly threw stones at "them owls" whenever they went past.

He mentioned it to the ever-vigilant Bossy Paterson that the eagles were important to him, that he had brought them from abroad at great trouble and expense and that he did not want them damaged by undisciplined village children. Bossy was delighted. It was another feather in his cap, another piece of business to become important about. Bossy guarded the eagles with more zeal that the squire had ever intended possible.

"He looked arter them owd owls," recalled Charlie, "as if he wore their mother. But that di'n't stop the boys. Cor, times they was chased away by owd Bossy. He'd hide up behind a hedge sometimes, a-waitin' for 'em. Silly owd fule — that only made it wuss. The boys they kep' shyin' stoons at the owd owls jist for the fun o' makin' Bossy run arter 'em. When the snow come there'd be a dozen kids — gals tew let alone boys — all throwin' these snowballs. Only snowballs worn't hard enough for some."

"Funny, that was. I allust useter go past them gates to

work, backards an' forrards. All that snow, o' course I cou'n't ride a bike, I atter walk. One arternoon, that was nigh on dark when I got to the gates an' I hap to stop jist there to light me pipe."

"I looked up an' — blow me — one o' them owls was gone. Haps another time I shou'n't ha' sin anythin' only I jist hap to look up, ow partner, same as yew might dew, an' there they were, only one on 'em had gone."

"Well, I went inside o' the gate jist curious to see if that owl was a-layin' there. That worn't but I see Tom Berry, the gardener, out o' the corner o' me eye sort o' hidin' in the bushes."

"One o' them owls is gone," I say, "an' I was jist lookin' to see if that had fell." Poor owd Tom — he say, 'Bossy ain't about, is he? 'Cos I got it here in a bag. My boy brought it down. He threw a grut owd brick at it — he shou'n't ha' done that. I don't know what I'm a-goin' to say when Bossy find out,' he say."

"Well," I say, "hev that hut it much?"

"No," he say, "that can be patched up agin all right but not afore tomorrer."

"Poor owd Tom, he was scared, him bein' gardener to the squire. So I say don't yew worry, Tom. Bossy'll be about in the mornin' no doubt, so as sune as that git dark yew git yar ladder an' bung a lot o' snow on top o' the posts so they look alike. Then yew git it patched up an' put it back tomorrer night. No one 'll know."

"Well, later on that night I sat aside o' my fire an' I thought: I'll hev a bit of a game with Bossy over this. So nex' mornin' I was at the gate early. I pushed all the snow off the post that Tom had put on an' yew could see right away there wor'n't no owl there."

"I'd got an owd sack I was carryin', with a couple o'

115

bricks in it an' as sune as Bossy come in sight I started to make off in a hurry as if I was guilty. Then he saw the owl was gone an' he started a-hollerin' but I kep' a-goin' an' he follered me all the way hoom. Course, he lived next to me then an' he di'n't want to accuse me till he was sartain sure I'd got the owl."

"So he kep' watch. I waited till I guessed Tom must ha' put the owl back on the post then I took the bag out o' the shed an' carried it to the barrer very sly as if I wanted to hide it. I knew Bossy was a—watchin'. I took the bag right up to the Hall pond and flung it in. Well, that di'n't go right in cos that was all frooz over. But Bossy did, tryin' to git it out. He was soppin' wet. He took the bag to the Hall door an' brought the squire out. I hid up an' listened.

"Tha's one o' your eagles, Bossy say to the squire, an' I know whew it was took it tew."

"Let's see what you've got afore you name any names, the squire say. He opened the bag an' course there wor'n't anything in 'cept a couple o' bricks. I'd a give anything to see Bossy's face: he never said another word — well, he cou'n't cos his teeth were chatterin' so."

"'We'll see if the eagle is really missing as you say, Paterson,' say the squire an' orf they go to the gate. Tom had put the eagle back in place by now an' Bossy stared as ef he was a-dreamin'. The squire wor'n't quite satisfied till he'd got a ladder an' he clumb up to hev a proper look."

"He must ha' sin where that'd bin repaired an' put back agin an' haps he guessed some o' the story but all he say was — 'I don't think these eagles are worth your spending valuable time on 'em,' he say, 'you come an' git what I owe you, Paterson, an' we'll call it a day.'"

"They was some rum goin's on in them days," concluded Charlie. "I never did see Bossy Paterson agin — but dew yew look at them gates as yew go, owd partner, see if them eagles ain't really owls."

Kaiser

During the cold spring the sown wheat stayed close to the earth. Kaiser watched it as he watched every single thing that occurred though it was not his farm. From the caravan sited in the lee of a high hedge, Kaiser noted the browning leaves in the easterly wind and the slow tillering. At that time he was no more than thirty years old and carried the odd nickname from his childhood years during the Great War though he had once been christened Edward.

He left the caravan and walked through the wheat no more yet than ankle high and came to the copse at the apex of the fields where the wind drove bitterly through the branches and beat back the surging life in the buds.

Here Kaiser came from time to time to survey the fields and watch the changing colour in the crops; here the farmer, George Warren, found him one day as he walked through from the farm lane. The two men stood together in the shelter of a group of beeches and looked and understood the same signs.

"Time this wind blow," Kaiser growled, "nothin'l move. That'll be a late harvest dew that last much longer."

The farmer chuckled. He was old — ahead of Kaiser by thirty years. "Things hev a way o' catchin' up — we may only lose the amount o' straw an' that don't worry me a mite. Y'know, I give up worryin' about late seasons long ago. I ain't come across a year yet that di'n't hev a harvest o' some sort."

Then he looked at Kaiser as he became serious, speaking of a matter that had long been on his mind.

"Yew waste tew much o' yar time botherin' 'bout this farm, Kaiser," he said bluntly. "No matter that it used to belong to yar family — that 'ont ever be yar farm agin. Time yew got used tew it."

Kaiser stared stubbornly across the fields. George went on, firmly but gently, for there were many things about this young man that he admired: "When I go, young Alec will take over. I know he ain't much of a farmer but I got this stake in the land so I could hand it on — an' arter all, he's my son."

Kaiser acknowledged the farmer's point of view by his silence but after a minute or two he said quietly: "This was my family's farm for nigh on two hundred year — till the depression come. From the time I was born I was brought up an' trained to be a farmer an' take over when it was my turn to inherit. A farm —" he hesitated, then went on: "A farm ain't jest what yew buy. There's other things — anyway, I reckon this farm still belong to me in a sense 'cause o' the two hundred years o' sweat my family put into it. They cared for it, built it up, ploughed their lives into the ground an' they buried their favourite animals togither in that odd-shaped little piece aside o' the hill."

The old farmer sighed. "I know how yew feel, Kaiser. I bought the farm durin' the depression when good land was goin' for only £5 an acre but that was long ago an' your father was glad to sell. Them days some farmers were jest walkin' out an' leavin their farms derelict. That was a fair price considering the risk."

"It ain't that — not the price," said Kaiser. "An' I got nothin' aginst yew — yew ha' bin very good to me. It's jest somethin' in me I can't turn my back on."

George Warren nodded in understanding and stepped forward to pick up a handful of wet, heavy soil. "Look at this," he told Kaiser. "This is what people dream about an' fight over, all over the world, but nobody ever really own it. Land. It's somethin' in a man's blood. Yet all a farmer 'mounts to is a caretaker. He look arter the land accordin' to his lights an' in the end all he's got to show is dirty boots."

He shivered and began to move. "Yew know why I'm tellin' yew this. When young Alec take over he may not take kindly to havin' yew around the place."

"I don't care ef he don't," retorted Kaiser. "That's all the more reason to stay — he ain't no farmer an' never will be."

"Well, it's only meant as a bit of friendly advice," George told him. "Now, don't yew hang around these owd woods an' git pneumonia."

As it happened, it was George Warren and not Kaiser who was taken to bed, perhaps from that very day when he had stood out in the bitter winds to talk to Kaiser. As he lay in the master bedroom of the old farmhouse the presence of Kaiser loomed largely in his waking dreams about the future of the farm and his family.

He remembered how, when he had first bought the farm, Kaiser had refused to move out with his family and how the boy's obstinacy had touched a chord in his own East Anglian temperament and he had recognised the need of Kaiser to stay on the land where he had been reared despite all reason.

He had given Kaiser a job and a caravan in which to live just beyond the orchard, knowing him to be a farmer as his own son would never be. From the caravan Kaiser came with complete willingness to work early and late with the men. Early on, he had been invited to take a room in the farmhouse but this Kaiser bluntly refused, never once setting foot in the house after his family had left. From the caravan, Kaiser watched. In off-duty hours in the cold light of early morning or the long, soft summer evenings Kaiser watched and had friendly converse with no one.

Lying ill in bed, George felt a growing apprehension at the ceaseless vigil that the younger man kept on the farm. If there was a loop-hole, the merest crack of an opportunity, then Kaiser would insert himself, lean and hungry as he was for the land. But all was safe, surely, with the title-deeds to be left in his ageing wife's name until Alec in turn would inherit.

All was safe — but he recalled the single-minded determination of the young boy to remain on the farm and knew the same fire burned in his desire to regain ownership. His concern increased when he heard that for the first time Kaiser had come to the house, had spoken to his wife and his daughter Mary. Apparently, the call was simply to put a courteous question as to the farmer's health and to express a wish for his recovery. The two women were charmed and delighted, having seen very little previously of this strange young man, and Mary, who had earlier felt rebuffed by Kaiser's attitude from any prospect of friendship, was flattered by his sudden attentions.

Kaiser, it seemed, was not only a farmer but a gentleman — albeit one who was swiftly falling in love. In his lonely bed, George heard the news and pondered. Why this sudden wooing of Mary when she and Kaiser had been the merest acquaintances for years? And what did he hope to gain by it? Certainly he could not come by ownership that way, though if he married Mary it would give him a right to stay on the farm.

When George's wife next came to the bedroom, he told her of his fears about Kaiser. She was older than George and ugly with bad temper. Long ago she had flowered as a village beauty but years of self-indulgent tantrums and peasant obstinancy had dulled her wits as well as her appearance.

"Why shou'n't he come after Mary?" she demanded. "He's a nice enough young man — I got nothin' against him."

"Because yew don't understand," fretted the old man. "Yew don't understand that there's on'y one thing mean anything to him in this world. Ef he's after Mary, tha's cos there's suffen else a-goin' on in his hid. Dew yew keep yar eye on him — I 'ont hev Mary used to satisfy his ambition."

So it was that, when Kaiser called again the old woman stayed in the kitchen with the couple, suspiciously at first then gradually becoming impressed by Kaiser's courtesy and thoughtfulness. Regularly until George died, Kaiser was in the house ready with sympathy and help and at the end he stood beside the bed with the family.

In his last moments George looked into Kaiser's eyes and saw the truth in the glint of triumph and realised too late the door he had left open for Kaiser to take the farm. Indeed, without a moment's pause, Kaiser turned from his courtship of Mary to a similar attention to the old crone, her mother.

They were married three months later despite all opposition. Between them were thirty years and a solid

122

bedroom wall and his hate and despair for having loved and then betrayed Mary; joining them together was the sour-sweet taste of victory and possession.

A Night To Forget

"Not a mark upon his body; not a stain upon his garment; his eyes staring glassily, stiff and cold."

So was George Mace found, long ago, on the steps of Breccles Hall, near Thetford and no one was ever able to tell how he met his death. There were some however, who blenched whenever his name was mentioned, who drank their pints up quickly and departed if someone tried to get at the truth of the matter in the bar of the local pub.

What they knew about George Mace's death did come out eventually, little by little, but for all its startling nature it only added to the mystery. What happened to Mace on that ghost-ridden night in Breccles Hall woods?

One thing everyone knew was that the dead man was a poacher who lived at Watton on the proceeds of his dangerous calling. Moreover, he was a man of some notoriety in the area as a leader of a whole gang of nocturnal predators. In those days of unassisted poverty the wealth of food existing on the inside of country estates was a challenge to hungry men. No matter that the dangers were immense — of wounding and mutilation by gun or mantrap, of prison and even deportation if caught, the insistence of empty stomachs demanded that the risk be taken.

Because large country estates were so fiercely patrolled and defended by gamekeepers, the poachers would often go in gangs — desperate men who would

124

fight and even kill if necessary when confronted. Such were the half-dozen hard-bitten local men who met secretly on that night in the outer plantations of Breccles Hall, with enough moonlight to show their way and help with their stealthy purposes. George Mace was instigator and leader of the raid. At his suggestion the gang split up into pairs, each pair going in a different direction but prepared to summon others if there was trouble. The plan agreed was that they would all return to the same spot in the plantation before the moon set in the early hours, in order to compare notes and share the spoils.

Moonlight illuminated the open spaces in the woods but threw dark shadows under the trees where gamekeepers could be waiting unseen with gun and dog. Mace pushed on steadily with his chosen partner, a former shoemaker named Joseph Lumb, but at some point or other they became separated in the darkness. Lumb dared not make a sound but waited for a little hoping to see his comrade's silhouette in the gloom. After a few minutes he continued alone, even more apprehensive and wary than before. It was he who came first to the appointed rendezvous, relieved to be out of the main danger area and more than satisfied with his haul. Soon the others returned — all except George Mace.

The poachers waited in uneasy silence, worried at their leader's absence, feeling a growing sense of calamity as the minutes went by. Two or three were frankly nervous and wanted to get home to hide their catch but Lumb insisted they wait for a reasonable time. The moon began to fade and the clearing where the men sheltered became black and cold. They dared not speak except in whispers and they could feel the awesome atmosphere of the woods creeping into their bones. What had happened to Mace?

In the acute silence at last there was a sound. But not here in the woods. It came from far down the driveway that led from the road to the Hall. It was not Mace by any manner of means — but a coach or carriage. The sound was of carriage wheels moving swiftly over the gravel. There was a great light, too. As the sound grew nearer so did the light that lit up the whole area and seemed to emanate from inside the carriage.

Almost numb with fear and astonishment, the waiting men moved closer to the drive. The carriage was moving at an immense speed and so brightly lit that the light flickered on the Hall windows and flooded the drive. Yet they could not see the coachman nor the horses nor hear anything but the carriage wheels. The fearful equipage continued to the very door of the Hall and there stopped. In the glow of light the men could see the steps of the carriage lowered then the carriage door opened. No one got out and the door of the Hall remained firmly shut. For about a minute the carriage door swung open then suddenly it was shut again and the spectral carriage continued on its way. The light gradually dimmed and the carriage disappeared.

In a panic of fear the poachers fled home and knew no sleep or rest till daylight came and showed the horror to other eyes. The body of George Mace lay still and composed and apparently untouched outside the door of Breccles Hall exactly where the ghostly coach had halted and there was nothing to tell of his end, except that "his eyes stared glassily, stiff and cold."

The Prowler

Little old Diller Bates, slight and small as if he had been specially made some seventy years before, to fit his dwarfish cottage, was always as punctual as a clock for the weekly institute meeting.

Every Thursday at ten minutes to seven he broke away from whatever diminutive domestic scene lay within and shuffled out of the door. Rain, hail or wind, he would appear at the gate, pulling his ancient muffler round his neck and muttering to himself as he set off down the road.

The content of his mutterings, which few people set themselves to listen to, was invariably caustic and irreverent and strangely enough, had little of Essex in it though he had lived in the village as long as most people could remember. Instead, it was of the slangiest cockney. Whitechapel could have welcomed him as a native but to the locals half of what he said was considered incomprehensible and required to be translated into the proper idiom and given with the accepted drawl.

It was just one of the things that caused Diller intense irritation and a good deal more muttering. The village people were 'balmy' he considered, and their failure to recognise his choice allusions and rhyming slang was 'habsolute hignorance'. The fact that he was secretary of the village Institute, a duty he pursued with bitter-tongued zeal, did nothing to melt his general disapproval.

Once on the way to the village hall, important with the

keys and the responsibility of locks and shutters, he was imbued with authority and early club members who might fall into step with him were likely to feel the rasping edge of his tongue. Generally, the 'club' dragged in slowly, so that after half an hour about a dozen of the village men had clumped into the timber hut and slammed up the lid of the stove to see how the fire was going.

The hall was still a novelty then. It had been built — such were the aspirations toward self-improvement at that time — with the fervent intention of providing a means of betterment for the lower orders. Among other things it was to be a reading-room. Once a week the rude intelligence of the village men was to be uplifted by sober books that would instruct but not corrupt.

So the Institute had begun. In the course of time a handful of rustics, less motivated by thoughts of Samuel Smiles than by the fact that this was the only place — bar the pub — where they could gather in the warm, obediently flipped through the improving manuals and marvelled at the pictures in the squire's old copies of Country Life. Literary interest, it had to be confessed, was limited and it stopped entirely when Ron Butters brought his mouth-organ and this stopped too when two or three members brought along playing cards.

The vicar, in charge of the Institute, was uneasy at the compromise. Playing at cards was hardly self-improvement at its best but surely better than nothing. So the men played cards or dominoes, told jokes and poked broad fun at each other's failings. Their wit was heavy but, at that particular time, edged with hostility and suspicion. From time to time during that winter a notorious prowler, a nocturnal Peeping Tom had been abroad in the village.

Not that anyone really knew anything about the prowler except by rumour. A good, clear sight of him was unknown but naturally so since the man, whoever he was, was swift and clever and melted completely into the darkness. Nevertheless, reports of his visitations were frequent and far-ranging and seemed to be genuine. It was impossible to say where he would be next.

A band of village men who had patrolled the gardens and lanes until midnight one night had been told the next morning that the man had been out again despite their vigilance. On the memorable evening of the following Thursday when the club assembled at the Institute the matter was heavy in their thoughts and bitter with suspicion.

It only took young Hoss Green to come into the hut at eight o'clock looking dishevelled and excited to stop every game of cards and dominoes on the spot. Hoss was breathless but informative. It was Mrs. Saunders this time, his next-door neighbour. She had gone out after dark to fetch the clothes from the line and there he was. He was pulling at the clothes till he saw her coming then somehow doubled up and disappeared. There was no doubting the story. He had seen himself how the clothes had been pulled and Mrs. Saunders had admitted there was a certain garment which she did not like to mention but which had entirely disappeared.

Perhaps at any other time the news would have been met by a good deal of guffawing and badinage but such was the feeling that no one made a sound. Hoss went on:

"What I done, sune as Mrs. Saunders towd me, round about six o'clock, what I done was to go to every house nearby an' see ef everyone was in who should be in. I bin to nigh on every house in the village an' every man fare to

129

be indoors and sittin' aside o' the fire — 'cept us lot. That stand to reason, I reckon, that this here bloke is from this village an' whoever he is — he's got to be one of us in this hall now."

Such was the suspicion among the men about the prowler that the idea produced an extravagant reaction. Men who had been partners in dominoes or whist a moment before now glared at each other, remembering earlier doubts and differences. Angry and frustrated, they began to jostle each other. A squabble broke out in the corner where Archie Pitt, a comparative new-comer to the village, found himself challenged by the towering Darkie Goldsmith. Tom Arkle was squaring up before his old enemy, Spider, whom he had always believed had robbed him of a setting of eggs three years before and Diller Bates was ready to fight anyone if only he were twenty years younger.

Nevertheless it was Diller who was first to see the nonsense of the situation and his belligerence turned to scorn at the 'hignorance' shown by some people. When the vicar appeared, something of decent behaviour was restored and Diller was saying that it was useless carrying on like that and accusing others without any proof. The thing was to find out who the guilty one was and if it was really someone present he knew of a certain-sure way how to do it.

He took the vicar aside and had a whispered consultation while the others waited. It was just a kind of confidence trick, Diller told the vicar. If he would simply return to the vicarage, see that the light was on over the porch and stand inside an unlighted room to check the names of the club members who passed the light, that would do the trick.

Then Diller turned to the group of waiting men and told them that the vicar had just informed him that someone in the village had actually seen the Peeping Tom and could identify him. The woman did not want to be known and would sit in the vicarage window in the dark. All the club members had to do to assure others of their innocence was to walk one by one under the light of the porch. The woman would give a signal if she saw the face she remembered and the prowler would be unmasked.

It was an elaborate and completely abortive trick. Only a devious foreigner like Diller would have thought of it. The theory was that all innocent club members would gladly pass under the light of the porch but that the guilty one would double back in the shadows so that he would not be seen. The watching vicar had only to tick off the names of those who appeared to be able to point out the single one who evaded the confrontation.

The charade was enacted at once and soon completed. Diller was confident, the others excited and noisy as they took their turn to walk by the vicarage porch. After half an hour the vicar came back with his list. No one had failed to appear.

Diller had to confess to his trick and such was the excitement of the hunt among the others that he might well have become the object of their aggression had not further news come of the elusive prowler at that very moment.

It was no less than old Martha Fry who poked her head in at the hut door, her bonnet askew, her voice high and querulous with indignation.

"Yew lot tergither," she squealed, "why ain't yew out an' lookin' fer that creature? Yew ought ter be ashamed o' yarselves, yew did, a-sittin' in here when there's folk bein' attacked in yar own village. Poor little owd Nellie up at the top housen, she ha' bin knocked over by this here bloke while yew so-called min sit here a-playin' games."

It was as good a match as any to set light to the men's growing need for action. They all but squashed poor Martha against the wall as they rushed out of the hut together to run the dark road to Nellie's place. Some of them picked up sticks on the way, others went off on a great surrounding strategy so that escape would be impossible. When they reached the top housen and Nellie's place they found the old woman still supported by her neighbours and loud in her grievance against whoever it was who bowled her into the hedge of lavender as he rushed out of the gate.

Excitement was intense as the men spread out into the neighbouring gardens knowing that their quarry must be in the vicinity. After a few minutes a moving figure was sighted in a shrubbery. It was Darkie Goldsmith who elected to go ahead, who saw and then tackled the shadowy figure, felt it escape from his clutching arms and forthwith sat down and watched it disappear.

There was no triumph in catching a goat, even if it was still chewing the missing pair of drawers.

A Swarm in June

You always knew what the shoemaker would say when you presented him yet again with your battered, gaping boots. "Them uppers are gone. That ain't a feasible job wi' them uppers gone."

As children we were never over-concerned about the uppers, what they were or where they were gone. Such things belonged to the knowing world of the adult and we always knew that the cobbler would patch the boots up somehow.

After all, boots were boots — it seemed a perfectly proper and natural use for them to kick anything that could be kicked and to scuffle around in the muddiest places until they could resist no more. When the toe-caps began to rear up and threaten to expose our toes or when the hole underneath could no longer be fobbed off with a piece of folded cardboard, then off we would have to go once more to ask the shoemaker if he 'could do anything with them.' For the hard, flinty roads that generally provided us with our playground, we always remembered to ask for toe and heel caps and plenty of Blakeys.

There was an equivalent amount of wear and tear at the other — physical — extreme. Boys wore hats, usually cloth caps, not casually but constantly as if it were something indecent to be seen without one. How could they do otherwise, when the common belief among their parents required that their heads needed protection from pneumonia in the winter and sunstroke in the summer?

In those days, if anyone were overcome by faintness or if they collapsed on a summer's day you could be pretty sure what caused it — sunstroke. It was sunstroke, no doubt about it, that affected poor Owd Tom who lived along the lane beyond the shoemaker's cottage though there were some who laughed and said mildly: "What, Owd Tom? Oh, he allus was a bit sorft. O' course, he make ut wuss hisself cos he never goo anywhere."

Owd Tom was not that old; the term was affectionate rather than descriptive. In the same way people meant that he was soft-hearted rather than soft in the head. All in all, it was as charitable a reputation as anyone could expect to earn from careful, rural neighbours. Folk had no grudge against Owd Tom.

As children, we often called to see Tom after visiting the cobbler. He lived in a timber bungalow on his own smallholding and one of the strange things about him by our own East Anglian standards was that he never asked you what you wanted there but took it for granted it was a courtesy call and went on with his endless, absorbing tasks with his stock or his crops.

Another habit, which sometimes made strangers tap their foreheads significantly, was that of addressing the animals that he kept around him and sometimes even his tools as if they were able to listen and understand. Owd Tom never seemed to be lonely or even alone, so close was he to the things he cared for — in fact it was we who used to go to the smallholding for comfort and recognition on those days when we felt despised and rejected.

Not that Tom had much time to waste on us. It required long hours of work to wring a subsistence from the holding, even by the basic, undemanding standards of the early twenties. Of the five acres, most was set aside for his pigs and goats and a mixed flock of hens that were fed by scraps and corn thrown from the kitchen door but there was an acre kept for potatoes and a bit of lucerne and there were several colonies of bees kept in old-fashioned skeps. There was also a donkey that pulled a small cart when required.

But this is making an orderly accounting of Tom's possessions where there was little enough order but plenty of delightful and casual confusion. Tom basked in his inefficiency without regret and only occasionally discouraged the encroaching tide of nature. Over all, there was a happy profusion that seemed to children like true wealth, though it was of a kind to provide very little profit to the man himself.

One day Owd Tom was standing at the tumbling gate that barely separated the poultry yard from the orchard. It was a warm June afternoon, quiet and luxuriantly sweet-smelling. Tom was engaged in making some direct and feeling remarks to the goats that were chewing at the drooping branches on the other side of the orchard.

"Yew duzzy owd fules, yew," he scolded loudly. "Yew know yew come hoom at foive. How'm I gorn to milk yew over there?" But the goats had found something that they liked and merely directed some withering looks at the old man as they chewed obstinately over a dribbling mouthful of greenstuff.

"I aren't a-comin' arter yew, that I dew know," Tom told them without malice. "I got other things to dew. Yew see ef I don't jest leave yew there an' git on — plenty other things to dew."

His words turned out to be immediately true. At that

very moment he heard and saw the swarm of bees. It came from the direction of his own hives and was massing and swirling as it gathered momentum over his head. For a moment he was at a loss, even for words. He had never before lost a swarm; he was surprised and mildly indignant.

"Ain't that a wonder?" he called out reprovingly, gazing upwards into the bright sunshine. "Ain't that a bloomin' wonder? Anyone 'd think I ha'nt took a mite o' care on ye, that they would. Stid o' that, I ha' fed ye an' sheltered ye — yes an' I towd ye."

He turned his eyes earthwards again and noticed one or two of us boys looking on. "I allust towd 'em," he repeated. So he had. Like many another country bee-keeper he had always informed the bees whenever there changes or events that he thought they should know about. It was supposed to keep the bees from swarming. But perhaps, unlike other bee-keepers, he had simply told them too much and they were off on a bewildered hunt for a more comprehensible master.

Owd Tom soon recovered himself — it was no time to be soliloquising. In a moment he had picked up a skep and a smoker and dived through one of the many gaps in his hedge as the swarm made raggedly for the church and rectory. When he caught up at last the bees had already been received, more or less, into the church. Not only had they settled upon a gargoyle above the porch but the rector was there below, already gloved and veiled and eager for capture.

The rector was a man of quite considerable size; a Cambridge rowing blue, a man not to be trifled with. Tom explained that the swarm had escaped from one of his own hives.

"I'm sure they have," said the big man. "But what is the law in the matter? If they come down in my grounds aren't they mine?"

"If yew can git 'em in yar hoive, I reckon so," agreed Tom.

"I'll get them. I've been waiting for two years for a good healthy swarm like this one."

As if to prove that such discussion was merely academic, the bees decided at that moment to leave the cold comfort of the gargoyle for more salubrious quarters, setting off in an agitated mass to fly right over the rectory roof.

"If they land on the Common," shouted the rector, "they belong to whoever can take them. May the best man win."

The bees did land on the Common, in the cluster of trees close by the bench that the parish council had put up after the Great War. The swarm was fairly high up and looked as if it would settle for the night. For the time being at least there was nothing that either man could do and they each retired with fitting dignity to their own homes.

By seven o'clock, however, Owd Tom had finished his chores and it was such a lovely evening that he welcomed the excuse to walk back down the lane and on to the Common. The rector was there, too. He had taken off his jacket and was sitting on the bench, stretching himself in the sun. The bees still clustered on a branch far above. Tom sat down beside the rector and after a time the village constable with off-duty bonhomie walked across and sat down and joined them in looking at the bees.

"I'll get them down for you," the man of action

137

decided. He went off and borrowed a clothes prop from the schoolmaster's garden where it usually held up a sagging branch of an apple tree. "Howd your skep underneath," he ordered. But Tom and the rector had no confidence in such tactics and were unwilling to do more than look on. The constable suddenly prodded the seething mass of bees and hastily withdrew. Several hundred close body-guards and personal friends of the queen made a concerted counter-attack and sent the constable, swiping and cursing with unheard-of oaths back to his own territory. The swarm stayed.

The rector and Owd Tom sat on. The evening was still warm but pearly and dim and so quiet that only the plop of a fish in the pond disturbed the even humming of the bees. Soon they were rejoined by the chastened constable and from time to time they looked up into the tree but somehow the swarm was no longer of any importance. Their low voices murmured across the Common as they talked of other summers and other swarms and remembered their youth and their early dreams. Then they became quiet again.

An old lurcher dog went limping across the Common towards the lane and momentarily disturbed the water hens. Then it was still again and a homely woman in a white apron came out of one of the cottages and stood looking for a few minutes before going in.

"We'll get the swarm tomorrow," they said but somehow knew that there would be no tomorrow like this. Today elements had come together and fused into something that held a hint of the real meaning of existence. When the shadows began to cross the Common and we who were then boys were called in to supper, the three men still sat contentedly together in the warm

138

silence, knowing, perhaps, that in the decades to come such a thing would not be possible again.

A Strange Story

It is doubtful if any ghost story could have more credible origins — no less than than the words of a sorrowing father, Sir Charles Lee, as told to the Bishop of Gloucester, both of them stern and godly men and unlikely to embellish the bare facts. Yet the story almost beggars belief.

It should be said first of all, that Sir Charles had already sustained a crushing grief in his life. Just over twenty years before this affair he had lost his young and lovely wife in giving birth to his only child, a daughter. It was a decision of affection for the baby girl rather than renunciation that caused him to hand her into the care of his sister, Lady Everard, to be brought up at Langleys, the family's country seat near Chelmsford. In the years that followed, Sir Charles saw his daughter regularly and she loved him dearly as indeed she did her aunt.

There is no evidence that Miss Lee was different from any other child and the records suggest that her childhood at Langleys was uncloudedly happy. As she came into the years that endowed her with beauty there were many who saw and admired, as much for her quality of natural goodness as for her looks. Whether she had, indeed, a secret sweetheart is something no one knows. All that is certain is that in accordance with the custom among the wealthy classes at that time, a marriage was arranged. As soon as she became of age she was to marry Sir William Perkins, carefully chosen from among her suitors and there is no evidence that Miss Lee was ever openly unhappy with the arrangement. However the wedding was never to take place.

At twenty years of age, made much of by her father and her aunt, Miss Lee seemed to be without a care in the world, enjoyed to the full the privileges of life in a great country house and showed no hint of the bizarre fate that was to befall her on a certain Thursday night in the year 1662.

That night Miss Lee had apparently just retired to bed when she thought she saw a light in her sitting room. Since she was always particular about such matters, she sent for her maid and asked why the light had been left burning. The maid replied that she had left no light, there was no light in the room and the only lighted candle in that part of the house was the one she carried with her.

It must have been the firelight, decided Miss Lee, but the maid shook her head. The fire had been out and cold for an hour or more. The only sensible explanation, the maid told her mistress, was that she had been half-asleep and dreamed about the light. Miss Lee, partly re-assured and determined not to give way to foolish fancies, agreed that it must be so and as soon as the maid left, she fell asleep.

At about two o'clock in the morning something disturbed her and she woke suddenly. There was the form of a youngish woman beside her bed. The apparition spoke to Miss Lee quietly, telling her that she was the spirit of her mother, that she was not to be frightened. She herself was quite happy and Miss Lee was to look forward to joining her and sharing her happiness — as she would do so before noon of this very day.

Again Miss Lee sent for her maid, who this time found

her mistress calmly dressing. When this was completed she went into her sitting room, shut the door and did not re-appear until nine o'clock, having spent that time in writing a long letter to her father. She then went down-stairs and handed the letter to her aunt, asking that it should be sent to her father as soon as she was dead. She behaved calmly and normally but in answer to her aunt's agitated questions insisted that she would soon die. Lady Everard could think of no better explanation than that her niece had suddenly lost her mind and sent post-haste to Chelmsford for doctors to come and see the girl.

This they did within an hour. Three doctors examined and conferred, let blood and looked wise but in the end had to confess they were baffled since Miss Lee seemed to be in the best of health and in good humour to boot.

With this over, Miss Lee asked that a chaplain might join them in prayer. At mid-morning, with the doctors still present, the chaplain looking on and all patently mystified, the music master arrived and Miss Lee took up her psalm-book and guitar as serenely as she would have on any other morning.

Yet this turned out to be no ordinary lesson. For about an hour she played and sang with such virtuosity that her teacher was astonished and those who listened were open-mouthed at such beautiful sounds. She did not pause until the clock approached the stroke of twelve. Then, without haste or apparent regret, she closed her book and carefully laid down the instrument, left the small chair which she had been sitting on and moved across the room to a larger chair. Here she composed herself, breathed deeply once or twice and died.

The letter that she had taken such trouble to write was sent at once to Sir Charles together with the news of her death. He was so deeply afflicted by grief that he could not bring himself to go to Langleys until after the funeral. Then, as she had requested in her letter, her body was removed to be placed beside her mother's body at Edmonton.

Little Farm Lost

Some of the material past of East Anglia, the historians say, lies buried under the sea. It may well be so, and they are entitled to mourn over lost churches and lost houses if they so wish. My own lament is for a farm, one of many farms, which is buried far from the coast and is lying under a great expanse of arable land. It is not some long-forgotten archeological site, either, but a farm that existed when I was a schoolboy.

It was the sort of farm that nowadays one only encounters in dreams. For one thing it was only of 53 acres and technically was scarcely a farm at all in size. Yet it had all the varied qualities of those days when the countryside was honeycombed with small farms and holdings. It was of course, 'mixed' and ingenuously unaware of such a thing as specialisation. It carried a stock of pigs and a few goats and four cows, with flocks of wandering hens and geese, all supported by small meadows of permanent grass and areas of arable crops that would seem laughably small and uneconomic by today's standards. On these 53 acres there were no fewer than 12 enclosures of land — tiny fields and paddocks of unending variety and interest, grouped about the farm house and buildings.

Of course, I cannot exactly pinpoint where the little farm now is, under the immaculate expanse of well-kept soil. Nor can I assert that the actual area — the 53 acres — has been lost or destroyed. On the contrary, I imagine that the same area now produces more in orthodox crops than ever it did as a separate farm. Nevertheless, that

144

farm is dead and all that it represented in terms other than crop production has been obliterated.

In the country, changes usually come slowly and almost unnoticed, so there is never a fixed point at which we can assess the new and say farewell to the old. Yet somehow, it is because the changes are so gradual that they are more complete. Slipping away like ghosts of old-style farming are the village ponds and the farm ponds, the friendly stiles and the flower-filled ditches, the corn-stacks and the cloud-high apple orchards and a dozen other rural sights once common but now lost in the modern style of farming.

So too, have disappeared innumerable small farms and smallholdings. Just for once, perhaps, we should put aside the logic of farm profits and mechanical efficiency and try to recall the quality of life that existed in the small scale before it was annihilated as a matter of expediency. Perhaps there is more to mourn here than in the ruins at the bottom of the sea, for few young people nowadays know the delight of tiny fields and paddocks enclosed by luxuriant hedges, of hens wallowing in the patches of unkempt nettles and goats munching through the forgotten apples in the long grass of the orchard. Few know the pleasure of walking through inefficient meadows of permanent grass — in East Anglia at any rate — where the buttercups and bull-daisies come up to the waist and there is always a lark singing overhead. Few experience the close domestic association with nature in which home and family and animals and growing things are all inextricably intertwined.

Supposing that one could make a kind of rough balance — not so much in terms of profit as in other benefits that the earth brings — between that small farm once provided and its present yield as an anonymous piece of land. Although my figures are purely speculative since they cannot ever be checked now, I would say that as a living entity that 53 acres once gave:

One mile of flourishing hedges and ditches, with nuts and sloes, bullaces and crab apples here and there for any to pick; perhaps 25 majestic trees; a hundred nests of considerable variety and untold legions of small-scale life; shelter, shade and windbreak; timber of all kinds; organic material constantly going back into the soil; farm animals in a free and natural environment.

All these — and for the family a simple and sparse living in freedom and independence. For children it was the happiest and the healthiest kind of life there could be. In total of all this wealth is the balm that it provides for the human spirit, even through there may be precious little in the bank.

By contrast, the same 53 acres, sans hedges, trees, buildings, stock and all other encumbrances, now sit blandly in an expanse of arable land with nothing to distinguish it nor even a clump of nettles for memorial. It grows corn as good as elsewhere, it requires a few hours attention each year from the big machines and at the end the total benefit lies in figures written down somewhere on paper. Everything else has vanished.

Five hundred small farms such as this disappeared in the 25 years after 1939 in Suffolk alone and no doubt the figures would be comparable throughout the rural area of East Anglia. Perhaps we should forget the ruins lying in theNorth Sea and shed a tear instead of a way of life that died with the small farm, and for a kind of countryman that we are not likely to meet again.

Sometimes I walk through familiar village lanes or

along the streets of my small home town, remembering the meeting places and corners where characters like Tommy Bowtrees, Cadger Green and Harry — whose other name I never knew — would have gathered but there is no one there, none of the old kind.

It was not always so. When I first came back to my native heath after some years in the neighbouring county, old Harry was the first familiar face that I encountered. He was standing in the street with his missus and they were looking in a shop window in which there were a few bowls of seed potatoes. They stood side by side, string bags drooping from their hands, and they spent an age comparing the varieties, no doubt remembering the yields and achievements, the successes and failures of years of contented potato growing, perhaps promising themselves to be bold and try a row or two of that new sort. If time moved on for other people that day, it certainly seemed to have no significance for them.

That was not many years ago and the shop window is still there. To be sure it is not now filled with bowls of potatoes but with modern aids to new kinds of gardeners — rooting powder and bags of compost and huge seed packets full of little else but promise. But Harry no longer looks in at the window. Nor can I find Cadger Green on the seat that he used to avow was his own, nor Winkle Pattison standing on the corner near his cottage. It puzzles and frets me. Where are all those whom I knew — the stalwart Gabriel Oaks whom I worked beside once on threshing drum and in the sugar-beet fields? They still live, I am sure, but have withdrawn their rare qualities from our public gaze. With them has gone the rich, good-natured idiom in which they used to put the local world to rights.

I can imagine Harry looking with me now at the shop window of the monster seed packets and tins of rooting powder.

"Blow me," he would say, "ef I di'nt buy one o' them grut owd packets last week. That took me near half a day to find the blessed seed — that was sech a mite. My wife she say why don't yew put yar ferret in next time."

Or, of the rooting powder he would say: "Y'know, I reckon owd Sam Fowler must ha' taken to that there powder when he was young. He properly take root when he set down."

But Harry is no longer around to make disparaging remarks in his independent way. If he lives he has lost his voice and his spirit. The people who go past the shop window now have no time to stop and no basic experience from which to criticise. They are of another context altogether, caught on hasty feet as they race to or from that most impatient mistress, the parked car or hurrying to keep a rendezvous with a television set.

To Harry and the others of my contemporaries there was no such compulsion. To walk was to stroll, free of puppet strings, ready to stare and to wonder. Only the countryman could afford to laugh at new-fangled ideas, since he was sure of his own steadfast values. Only the countryman could pick out the ersatz and the humbug from a hundred yards away and dispose of in the idiom of honest contempt. Where is he now — for who now laughs at the ersatz?

And who now uses the gentle dialect in the idiom of kindness and affection? Harry's grandson was always "my little owd mate" and his wife "my owd dare." At his door you would always hear: "Dew yew come in, owd pardner. Don't yew stand out there in the cold." It is

148

many years since I head the warm comfort of being called "owd pardner."

Sometimes, when I puzzle over the disappearance of such old friends, I get to wondering whether by some dreadful sci-fi trick they have become transmogrified by the wash of new-mannered folk that has flooded East Anglia into a kind of bland, pale copy of people they once were.

Perhaps they have become smooth and faceless and uncritical, joining the endless scurry between supermarket and car park. I cannot think it is possible but it would be a great reassurance to me if just now and again above the twittering of strange voices I could hear the unmistakeable sound of my "owd pardners" amiably reducing the affectations of the the local world to a proper proportion.